Social Security Sense

For those age 60 to 70

By Dana Anspach

aBM

Published by:

A Book's Mind
PO Box 272847
Fort Collins, CO 80527

www.abooksmind.com

Copyright © 2016 Dana Anspach

ISBN: 978-1-944255-05-3

Library of Congress Control Number: 2017936373

Printed in the United States of America

"We can never insure one-hundred percent of the population against one-hundred percent of the hazards and vicissitudes of life. But we have tried to frame a law which will give some measure of protection to the average citizen and to his family against the loss of a job and against poverty-ridden old age."

-Franklin D. Roosevelt

Contents

Disclosures

About the Author

Since 2008, Dana Anspach has been writing for About.com as their Money-Over55 Expert. You are welcome to sign up for her free weekly newsletter on the About.com MoneyOver55 site. She also contributes to MarketWatch as one of their RetireMentors.

Anspach has been practicing as a financial planner since 1995, and founded Sensible Money, LLC, in 2011. Sensible Money is a registered investment advisory firm in Scottsdale, Arizona, with a developed specialty in the area of retirement income planning (www.sensiblemoney.com).

Dana is a Certified Financial Planner, Retirement Management Analyst, a Kolbe Certified Consultant, and a member of NAPFA (National Association Of Personal Financial Advisors), FPA (Financial Planning Association), and an active member of RIIA (Retirement Income Industry Association).

As an expert in her field, she has spoken for numerous organizations, associations, and conferences on the topic of retirement planning and interacts regularly with readers and clients on these topics. Anspach believes the retirement income planning process is not static; it is alive with choices and variables. To make the best decisions, consumers need a way to understand the interactions of the choices they make and the corresponding impact on their future. To trust the information they see, they need an independent voice that provides information free of the influence of politics, financial products, or media articles that are advertising in disguise. As her clients can tell you, Dana Anspach is that independent voice.

Note From the Author

Some of you have been following my work for years. Thank you for all your kind words. And thank you to those of you who take the time to send corrections. If you spot a potential error, feel free to email me at moneyover55@gmail.com with the subject line "SSS book correction".

It takes an entire team of people to proof a book that has technical information. We have done our best to make sure everything is accurate but there can be no guarantee that we have not made errors. And of course the laws and rules can change at any time.

I believe Social Security should be claimed as part of a plan – it should not be a decision made in isolation. With that in mind remember I don't know your personal circumstances. Nor does any journalist, TV or radio commentator. Nor can I offer advice or recommendations via email.

It is up to you and your financial or tax advisors to determine a final course of action that is appropriate after considering not only your financial circumstances, but also your values and beliefs.

My goal is to arm you with accurate information so that when it comes time to choose a course of action, the choice you make will be an informed one.

Acknowledgements

To my first financial planner, Les Zetmeir. You started it all. You showed me what financial planning is really all about.

Joe Elsasser, I cannot thank you enough for promptly answering all my Social Security questions and taking the time to explain things to me. You are a Social Security saint. And to you and your team the speed at which you were able to update your software to reflect the new Social Security rules was astonishing and was a huge help to those of us who needed to quickly see how the changes might affect our clients. Amazing stuff.

Larry Kotlikoff, thank you for all of our conversations, for allowing me to run scenarios using your software, and most of all for encouraging me to continue my work.

To my team at Sensible Money; Jody Hulsey, Brian Duvall Kathy Mealey, Chuck Robinson, Suzanne Nagel, and Michelle Buonincontri - I could not have completed this without you. Thank you for your support, hard work, and for your amazing dedication to our clients. Brian thank you for your detailed review of my calculations. I wouldn't want to write something like this without you there to review it.

Introduction

Since 2008 I have been writing an online advice column called MoneyOver55. At my first annual review my editor asked me to write more content about Social Security. I began reading everything I could find on the topic and writing as much as I could about it. It soon became my most popular topic.

As I added content, readers began asking me questions. Many questions I receive are from informed readers who are trying to employ a suggestion in one of my articles, but when they go to the Social Security office they are told they cannot do what I say they can do. They write to me asking for a link to the source of my information. I send them back a link to Social Security's own website. I love it when they share their stories with me. This was a thank you note I received from one reader,

> "Dana,
>
> Just wanted to let you know the outcome. The Soc. Sec. administration is letting me take my own (very modest) retirement benefit now at age 62, with the understanding that I'll switch to the much larger widow's benefit when I turn 66. They've started sending me the checks already. They didn't give me any trouble at all, to my surprise and relief. I went in there prepared to do battle, which proved unnecessary, but the fact that I arrived armed with information made me feel very comfortable and prepared. Thanks for your help!"

The claiming plan employed by this widow is still viable today, yet many widows and widowers remain unaware of the rules and get less lifetime income than they otherwise might have. You, dear reader, can help change this by passing the knowledge you're about to learn on to others.

If you know the rules you can accomplish whatever the law allows. Knowing the rules is key. Below is another thank you note I received from a reader who was also able to accomplish what she wanted – but it took persistence on her part.

"Dana,

I just wanted to thank you again for your reference. I signed up for Social Security today based on my husband's benefits and will leave mine to accumulate. So you were right. And a note, the guy at Social Security said he has been working there for 25 years and never heard of this. At first he said I was wrong, as did his supervisor, but after reading his own website (from your reference), and talking to the regional management, he agreed that I had a choice and it got done. Thanks for your help."

The claiming plan employed by this second reader will only be available for another few years.

How Quickly Things Change

On Nov. 2, 2015 new laws[1] were put in place that affect Social Security claiming options. This book covers both the old and new laws.

Due to the new laws the option described in the second quoted email exchange will not be available for anyone who turns age 62 on or after January 2, 2016.

Claiming options will become slightly simpler for couples where both halves reach age 62 in 2016 or later, but in the interim, it is more important than ever to evaluate your claiming choices.

Those of you who reach(ed) the age of 62 by year end 2015 will want to examine your Social Security claiming options carefully. And please, pass the word along to anyone else who may be able to benefit.

The rules are far more complex than a glance at your Social Security statement would lead you to believe.

Making an uninformed choice can mean less income for the rest of your life, and for many of you, the decision as to when to begin your Social Security benefits will be one of the biggest financial decisions you ever make.

Chapter 1
What Your Benefits Are Worth

What would you guess your Social Security benefits are worth; a few hundred thousand, maybe? Would it surprise you to know that the average single person living twenty five years could receive $500,000 or more in total Social Security benefits? Many married couples will receive over a million dollars in total benefits. It's a big pot of money. By making a wise decision, you can increase the size of the pot.

According to the Social Security office, in 2014 the average monthly Social Security retirement benefit was $1,329 a month[2]. That's $15,948 a year. Starting in 1975, Social Security benefits have a cost-of-living adjustment applied to them, which means your benefits increase as prices rise (prices as measured by the Consumer Price Index, called the CPI-W[3]).

Historically benefits have increased at an annual rate in excess of 3.5%, although in recent years 2012 – 2015 increases have been less than 2% a year. If you take your $15,948 a year increasing at 2% a year for 25 years, you would be expected to receive $510,819 in total benefits.

People miss out on thousands in benefits because they talk to a neighbor, friend, family-member, well-meaning but uninformed accountant or financial advisor, or even the Social Security office – all who, unintentionally, give them bad advice.

The decision as to when to start your Social Security benefits has been examined by academics from numerous possible angles, and there is overwhelming evidence that for most people taking benefits at the earliest possible claiming age is not the wisest choice.

Let's look at a simple example. We'll use a hypothetical couple, Sam and Sara. Sam reached age 66 in 2015. Sara reached age 62 in 2015.

You can see Sam and Sara's possible monthly Social Security benefit amounts in Table 1-1. These amounts assume that Sara has no more earnings after age 62, and that any earnings Sam has after age 66 are not large enough to increase his future benefit amount.

Table 1-1. Sam and Sara Social Security Benefits, no inflation adjustments		
Age	Sam	Sara
62	$-	$910
66	$2,173	$1,214
70	$2,868	$1,602

The amounts in Table 1-1 reflect what you might see on your Social Security statement.

Sara looks at these numbers and thinks about her mom, who lived to 93. She thinks it is quite likely she'll live to 90 or beyond. Sara decides to do a simple calculation to see what amount of total dollars she will receive from Social Security over the next 28 years, which would get her to her 90th birthday.

- If she starts benefits at 62, and lives to 90, she'll get $10,920 a year for 28 years for a total of $305,760 (not including inflation increases).

- If she starts at 70, and lives to 90, she'll get $19,224 a year for 20 years for a total of $384,480 (not including inflation increases).

Common sense tells you if you are getting more total income from Social Security that means less of your own money you have to spend to have the same lifestyle.

Suppose Sara needs $25,000 a year total. Initially, like most people, she wants to take Social Security early.

- If she does, as stated she gets $10,920 a year, which means she'll need to withdraw $14,080 a year from savings. Over 28 years that's $394,240 of withdrawals from savings.

- If she waits to take Social Security until age 70, in her first eight years she must withdraw the full $25,000 a year from savings for a total of $200,000. Then for the remaining 20 years she only needs to withdraw $5,776 a year ($25,000 needed minus the $19,224 of Social Security starting at age 70) for a total of $115,520. Her total withdrawals are $315,520.

- The difference between those two numbers is $78,720.

Conclusion: by delaying the start date of her Social Security, Sara gets to spend the exact same amount, $25,000 a year, but needs to use less of her own savings to do it.

For those collecting benefits in 2015[4]:

Social Security provided 90% or more of their total income for 22% of marrieds and 47% of singles.

Social Security provided 50% or more of their total income for 53% of marrieds and 74% of singles.

Yes, But...

The previous calculations do not take into account the fact that Sara's savings will be earning something. If she delays Social Security she will have to spend down her savings more rapidly and will miss out on what is called the opportunity cost – the rate of return that her savings could have earned.

If Sara must use up her own savings for eight years while she delays the start of her Social Security, that is eight years that her savings will not be earning interest.

Sara believes an investment portfolio can earn 5% a year or more. She puts together a set of calculations (shown in Table 1-2 and Table 1-3) and determines that if she starts Social Security at 62, and withdraws the difference from her $400,000 of savings that is earning 5% a year, by the end of the year that she reaches age 89 she will still have $704,628 remaining[5]. Wow!

If she starts Social Security at 70, she must withdraw $25,000 a year from her savings for the first eight years. She determines that by end of the year that she reaches 89 she would still have $702,427 in the bank. This is $2,201 less than if she had started Social Security at age 62. However for every year past 90 that she lives, she sees that she ends up with more funds remaining if she starts Social Security at 70 instead of 66.

Table 1-2. Sara's Savings After Withdrawal if She Starts SS at 62 – no inflation				Starting balance: $400,000
Age	Income Needed	(less) SS benefit	(equals) gap that is withdrawn	Value after withdrawal, growing at 5%
62	$25,000	$10,920	$14,080	$405,216
63	$25,000	$10,920	$14,080	$410,693
64	$25,000	$10,920	$14,080	$416,443
65	$25,000	$10,920	$14,080	$422,482
66	$25,000	$10,920	$14,080	$428,822
67	$25,000	$10,920	$14,080	$435,479
68	$25,000	$10,920	$14,080	$442,469
69	$25,000	$10,920	$14,080	$449,808
70	$25,000	$10,920	$14,080	$457,515
71	$25,000	$10,920	$14,080	$465,606
72	$25,000	$10,920	$14,080	$474,103
73	$25,000	$10,920	$14,080	$483,024
74	$25,000	$10,920	$14,080	$492,391
75	$25,000	$10,920	$14,080	$502,226
76	$25,000	$10,920	$14,080	$512,554

77	$25,000	$10,920	$14,080	$523,397
78	$25,000	$10,920	$14,080	$534,783
79	$25,000	$10,920	$14,080	$546,739
80	$25,000	$10,920	$14,080	$559,291
81	$25,000	$10,920	$14,080	$572,472
82	$25,000	$10,920	$14,080	$586,312
83	$25,000	$10,920	$14,080	$600,843
84	$25,000	$10,920	$14,080	$616,101
85	$25,000	$10,920	$14,080	$632,122
86	$25,000	$10,920	$14,080	$648,945
87	$25,000	$10,920	$14,080	$666,608
88	$25,000	$10,920	$14,080	$685,154
89	$25,000	$10,920	$14,080	$704,628
Sum	$700,000	$305,760	$394,240	

Table 1-3. Sara's Savings After Withdrawal if She Starts SS at 70– no inflation				Starting balance: $400,000	Diff. between ending balance in Table 1-2
Age	Income Needed	(less) SS benefit	(equals) gap that is withdrawn	Value after withdrawal, growing at 5%	Over/Under
62	$25,000	$0	$25,000	$393,750	-$11,466
63	$25,000	$0	$25,000	$387,188	-$23,505
64	$25,000	$0	$25,000	$380,297	-$36,147
65	$25,000	$0	$25,000	$373,062	-$49,420
66	$25,000	$0	$25,000	$365,465	-$63,357
67	$25,000	$0	$25,000	$357,488	-$77,991
68	$25,000	$0	$25,000	$349,112	-$93,356
69	$25,000	$0	$25,000	$340,318	-$109,490
70	$25,000	$19,224	$5,776	$351,269	-$106,245
71	$25,000	$19,224	$5,776	$362,768	-$102,838
72	$25,000	$19,224	$5,776	$374,841	-$99,261
73	$25,000	$19,224	$5,776	$387,519	-$95,505
74	$25,000	$19,224	$5,776	$400,830	-$91,561
75	$25,000	$19,224	$5,776	$414,807	-$87,420
76	$25,000	$19,224	$5,776	$429,482	-$83,072

77	$25,000	$19,224	$5,776	$444,891	-$78,506
78	$25,000	$19,224	$5,776	$461,071	-$73,712
79	$25,000	$19,224	$5,776	$478,060	-$68,679
80	$25,000	$19,224	$5,776	$495,898	-$63,393
81	$25,000	$19,224	$5,776	$514,628	-$57,844
82	$25,000	$19,224	$5,776	$534,295	-$52,017
83	$25,000	$19,224	$5,776	$554,945	-$45,898
84	$25,000	$19,224	$5,776	$576,627	-$39,474
85	$25,000	$19,224	$5,776	$599,394	-$32,729
86	$25,000	$19,224	$5,776	$623,299	-$25,646
87	$25,000	$19,224	$5,776	$648,399	-$18,209
88	$25,000	$19,224	$5,776	$674,754	-$10,400
89	$25,000	$19,224	$5,776	$702,427	-$2,201
Sum	$700,000	$384,480	$315,520		
If Sara lives longer...					
90	$25,000	$19,224	$5,776	$731,483	$6,408
91	$25,000	$19,224	$5,776	$761,993	$15,448

Although she realizes she could live past 90, age 90 seems quite far away to Sara. Why shouldn't she just take Social Security at 62?

Sara knows that she is not a finance expert and before making a decision she decides to have someone check her calculations. She turns to her sister, Sally, who is a finance professor at a university.

Sally looks at Sara's analysis and quickly sees a key ingredient that is missing.

Sara made a common mistake – she did her calculations using the numbers on her Social Security statement without accounting for inflation.

Adding in Inflation

The numbers you see on your Social Security statement do not show you what your benefit will be with the cost of living increases that will be applied.

Assuming a 2% cost of living increase, here are the respective benefits Sam and Sara would actually get should they delay and claim past their ages 66 and 62.

Table 1-4. Sam and Sara Social Security Benefits, with 2% inflation		
Future benefit estimates were calculated using Social Security Timing® software.		
Age	**Sam**	**Sara**
62	$-	$910
66	$2,173	$1,313
70	$3,104	$1,876

Sara decides to redo her calculations (shown in Table 1-5 and Table 1-6). This time she calculates inflation adjusted income amounts each year from now until her age 90 and adds them up.

- Assuming her age 62 benefit increases at 2% a year from 62 through age 90 she'll receive a cumulative $404,448 [6].

- If she starts at 70 she'll receive a cumulative $546,936.

- This is a difference of $142,488.

As mentioned, Sara has $400,000 saved. Now that she has added inflation adjustments she decides to take a fresh look at her calculations to see how much savings she will have left depending on what age she claims her Social Security.

She projects her investment balance and again assumes it earns 5% a year. In one projection (shown in Table 1-5) she subtracts out the difference between the $25,000 a year she needs, and the amount she would get if she claims at 62. She remembers to inflate her needed $25,000 each year by 2%.

In another projection (shown in Table 1-6) she subtracts out the full $25,000 a year for eight years, then after 70 only subtracts out the difference between the inflation adjusted $25,000 a year she needs, and the amount she would get once she began benefits at age 70.

Here's what she sees.

- If she claims at 62, by the end of the year she turns 89, she would have $493,966 left.

- If she claims at age 70 by the end of the year she turns 89 she would have $581,073 left.

- The difference is $87,107.

Table 1-5. Sara's Savings After Withdrawal if She Starts SS at 62 – inflation adjusted			Starting balance: $400,000
Age	Income Needed	(less) SS benefit	(equals) gap that is withdrawn	Value after withdrawal, growing at 5%
62	$25,000	$10,920	$14,080	$405,216
63	$25,500	$11,136	$14,364	$410,395
64	$26,010	$11,364	$14,646	$415,536
65	$26,530	$11,592	$14,938	$420,628
66	$27,061	$11,820	$15,241	$425,656
67	$27,602	$12,060	$15,542	$430,620
68	$28,154	$12,300	$15,854	$435,504
69	$28,717	$12,540	$16,177	$440,293
70	$29,291	$12,792	$16,499	$444,984
71	$29,877	$13,044	$16,833	$449,558
72	$30,475	$13,308	$17,167	$454,010
73	$31,084	$13,572	$17,512	$458,323
74	$31,706	$13,848	$17,858	$462,488
75	$32,340	$14,124	$18,216	$466,486
76	$32,987	$14,400	$18,587	$470,294

77	$33,647	$14,688	$18,959	$473,902
78	$34,320	$14,988	$19,332	$477,299
79	$35,006	$15,288	$19,718	$480,460
80	$35,706	$15,588	$20,118	$483,358
81	$36,420	$15,900	$20,520	$485,980
82	$37,149	$16,212	$20,937	$488,296
83	$37,892	$16,536	$21,356	$490,287
<u>84</u>	$38,649	$16,872	$21,777	<u>$491,935</u>
85	$39,422	$17,208	$22,214	$493,206
86	$40,211	$17,556	$22,655	$494,079
87	$41,015	$17,904	$23,111	$494,516
88	$41,835	$18,264	$23,571	$494,492
89	<u>$42,672</u>	<u>$18,624</u>	<u>$24,048</u>	$493,966
Sum	$926,280	$404,448	$521,832	

Table 1-6. Sara's Savings After Withdrawal if She Starts SS at 70 – inflation adjusted				Starting balance: $400,000	Over/Under compared to age 62
Age	Income Needed	(less) SS benefit	(equals) gap that is withdrawn	Value after withdrawal, growing at 5%	
62	$25,000	$0	$25,000	$393,750	-$11,466
63	$25,500	$0	$25,500	$386,663	-$23,732
64	$26,010	$0	$26,010	$378,685	-$36,851
65	$26,530	$0	$26,530	$369,763	-$50,865
66	$27,061	$0	$27,061	$359,837	-$65,819
67	$27,602	$0	$27,602	$348,847	-$81,773
68	$28,154	$0	$28,154	$336,727	-$98,777
69	$28,717	$0	$28,717	$323,411	-$116,883
70	$29,291	$22,512	$6,779	$332,463	-$112,521
71	$29,877	$22,968	$6,909	$341,831	-$107,727
72	$30,475	$23,424	$7,051	$351,519	-$102,491
73	$31,084	$23,892	$7,192	$361,543	-$96,780
74	$31,706	$24,372	$7,334	$371,920	-$90,569
75	$32,340	$24,852	$7,488	$382,653	-$83,833
76	$32,987	$25,356	$7,631	$393,773	-$76,521

77	$33,647	$25,860	$7,787	$405,286	-$68,616
78	$34,320	$26,376	$7,944	$417,209	-$60,089
79	$35,006	$26,904	$8,102	$429,563	-$50,897
80	$35,706	$27,444	$8,262	$442,365	-$40,993
81	$36,420	$27,984	$8,436	$455,626	-$30,355
82	$37,149	$28,548	$8,601	$469,376	-$18,919
83	$37,892	$29,112	$8,780	$483,626	-$6,661
84	$38,649	$29,700	$8,949	$498,411	$6,476
85	$39,422	$30,288	$9,134	$513,740	$20,534
86	$40,211	$30,900	$9,311	$529,650	$35,571
87	$41,015	$31,512	$9,503	$546,155	$51,638
88	$41,835	$32,148	$9,687	$563,291	$68,799
89	$42,672	$32,784	$9,888	$581,073	$87,106
Sum	$926,280	$546,936	$379,344		

Sara plays around with her numbers and determines that if she lives to age 90, after all fees and expenses, she would have to earn a rate of return on her savings slightly higher than 7%[7] for the age 62 claiming choice to work out better than the age 70 choice.

Sara takes her new analysis back to her sister to Sally for a final review. Sally looks at it and suggests there is one other factor that Sara might want to consider. Sally explains that a dollar today is worth more than a dollar in the future.

In order to compare a future outcome, you need to translate that into what it is worth in terms of money in the bank today. To do that you use a math concept called present value.

Who Benefits from Delaying Social Security?

"The gains from delaying are greater at lower interest rates, for married couples relative to singles, for single women relative to single men, and for two-earner couples relative to one-earner couples."

-The Decision to Delay Social Security Benefits: Theory and Evidence by John B. Shoven, Sita Nataraj Slavov, NBER Working Paper No. 17866, February 2012

Present Value

The present value formula can be used to calculate the amount of money you need in the bank today, earning a specified rate of return, so that it will have enough gains to meet a future expense (or a series of future expenses).

For example, if you have a $200,000 expense ten years from now, below is the present value (what you would have to have in the bank today) based on various assumed rates of return:

- 3%, $148,818
- 4%, $135,112
- 5%, $122,782

If you had $135,112 in the bank today and you could be assured it would earn an annual 4% rate of return, it would be worth $200,000 ten years from now.

I did the calculations on an HP12C calculator. Entries to do this are:

- n = 10
- i = rate of return (i.e. 4% in the example)
- PMT = 0
- FV = $200,000
- Then hit PV to solve for present value

This simple present value calculation shows you that the higher the rate of return, the lower the amount needed today to fund the future expense.

In order to have the potential to earn higher rates of return, you must take on additional risk. Sally the finance professor explains to Sara that Social Security has a risk level that is equivalent to other safe investments, like FDIC insured certificates of deposit, or U.S. Treasury Bills. An investment portfolio will deliver a variable return, Sally explains, not a stable consistent return.

To do an apples-to-apples comparison, Sally suggests that Sara calculate the present value of each of her Social Security claiming choices by discounting the income stream back to today's value using a rate of return equivalent to a safe investment[8] .

Sara thinks about this and decides to use a return of 3%. She knows that today she may not be able to earn 3% from safe investments, but in the past she would have been able to earn more than this and she thinks over the next 20 – 30 years it is likely to average about 3%. She decides to do some additional calculations.

In Table 1-7 you see Sara's inflation adjusted Social Security benefits at age 62, and at age 70.

At age 62, her $10,920 of benefits are worth $10,920. But next year's $11,136 of benefits are worth only $10,812 in today's dollars when using a 3% discount rate. Meaning it takes $10,812 in the bank earning 3% to deliver $11,136 of income in one year.

This 3% discount rate means we are assuming that over time Sara can earn a 3% rate of return on safe investments with a risk level similar to the guaranteed nature of Social Security payments.

Table 1-7. Present Value of Sara's Benefits

Age	SS benefit @ 62	PV of benefits @ 3%	Cumulative sum of PV	SS benefit @ 70	PV of benefits @ 3%	Cumulative sum of PV
62	$10,920	$10,920	$10,920	--	--	--
63	$11,136	$10,812	$21,732	--	--	--
64	$11,364	$10,712	$32,443	--	--	--
65	$11,592	$10,608	$43,052	--	--	--
66	$11,820	$10,502	$53,554	--	--	--
67	$12,060	$10,403	$63,957	--	--	--
68	$12,300	$10,301	$74,258	--	--	--
69	$12,540	$10,196	$84,454	--	--	--
70	$12,792	$10,098	$94,552	$22,512	$17,771	$17,771
71	$13,044	$9,997	$104,549	$22,968	$17,603	$35,374
72	$13,308	$9,902	$114,451	$23,434	$17,430	$52,804
73	$13,572	$9,804	$124,256	$23,892	$17,260	$70,064
74	$13,848	$9,713	$133,969	$24,372	$17,094	$87,158
75	$14,124	$9,618	$143,587	$24,852	$16,923	$104,081
76	$14,400	$9,520	$153,107	$25,356	$16,763	$120,844
77	$14,688	$9,428	$162,534	$25,860	$16,599	$137,443
78	$14,988	$9,340	$171,874	$26,376	$16,437	$153,880
79	$15,288	$9,249	$18,124	$26,904	$16,277	$170,157
80	$15,588	$9,156	$190,280	$27,444	$16,120	$186,277
81	$15,900	$9,068	$199,348	$27,984	$15,959	$202,236
82	$16,212	$8,976	$208,324	$28,548	$15,806	$218,043
83	$16,536	$8,889	$217,213	$29,112	$15,649	$233,692
84	$16,872	$8,805	$226,018	$29,700	$15,500	$249,192
85	$17,208	$8,719	$234,737	$30,288	$15,347	$264,539
86	$17,556	$8,636	$243,374	$30,900	$15,201	$279,739
87	$17,904	$8,551	$251,925	$31,512	$15,050	$294,790
88	$18,264	$8,469	$260,394	$32,148	$14,907	$309,697
89	$18,624	$8,384	$268,778	$32,784	$14,759	$324,455

The year Sara turns 81, the present value of her Social Security payments if she begins at age 70 exceed the present value of her income stream if she begins benefits at 62.

By the end of the year in which she turns age 89 the difference between the two choices is $55,677. This means if she lives to 90 or longer starting benefits at age 70 is worth $55,677 more than starting benefits at age 62. In other words, claiming later is like having an additional $55,677 in the bank at age 62.

Sara verifies this with Sally and Sally confirms that comparing the two options on a present value basis using a rate of return reflective of the guaranteed nature of Social Security is the mathematically correct way to compare these options.

Sara also notices that at age 75, if she claims at 62 she will be getting $14,124 - but if she waits until 70 to begin benefits by the time she reaches 75 she will be getting $24,852. The thought of having almost $25,000 a year of guaranteed income at that age is comforting to her.

Sara has now projected her options in every way she can think of. Here is a summary of what she calculated.

- If she calculates benefits without inflation, for each year she lives past age 90, claiming later is to her benefit.

- If she considers inflation and a 5% growth rate on investments by the time she reaches 84 the later claiming choice is the one that leaves her with more money in the bank.

- In the long run in order for her age 62 claiming choice to work best she would have to earn a 7% return after all fees and expenses, each year from age 62 on. (History shows this is far from a sure thing.)

- If she compares the two income streams out to the end of the year she reaches 89, on a present value basis claiming at 70 is like having an extra $55,677 in the bank today.

- By delaying the start of her benefit at age 75 she will have an additional $10,728 a year of guaranteed income.

Although it is scary, she sees the value in starting benefits at a later age. She can see how that choice offers more certainty, and provides greater security later in life.

Sara wants to show her calculations to Sam, her husband. First, however she decides to read up about the Social Security rules. She wants to do all her homework before presenting Sam with her conclusion.

Let's take a look at the Social Security basics that Sara learns about.

Chapter 2
Social Security Basics

If I could administer a quiz before allowing people to begin their benefits, I would. The point of the quiz would be to make sure people weren't unknowingly making a decision that would hurt them financially. My quiz would cover all the basic items below:

- Your benefit amount is determined by your highest 35 years of indexed earnings, and the age at which you begin benefits (Indexed earning are covered in the Appendix.)

- You can begin taking your Social Security benefits as early as age 62, but you will receive a reduced benefit amount if you do so.

- You receive your full benefit amount at your Full Retirement Age (FRA), which varies by your year of birth. For those born January 2, 1943 to January 1, 1955 your FRA is 66. (Note, unless it is used as a direct quote throughout this text I have chosen to capitalize "Full Retirement Age" or use "FRA" so you know I am referring to the technical age determined by your date of birth.)

- You can receive the maximum monthly benefit amount by waiting until age 70 to begin benefits. The increases you receive by delaying benefits between your FRA and age 70 are referred to as delayed retirement credits.

- If you begin benefits before you reach your FRA and you continue to work, your Social Security benefits will be reduced if you earn too much. This reduction in benefits no longer applies once you reach your FRA.

- Your Social Security benefits are subject to income taxes based on a formula that takes into account other sources of income you have.

- If you are married, when you begin your own benefits it will affect your spouse's ability to claim a spousal benefit, and vice versa. It will be important to understand the claiming combinations available as a married couple before either one of you start receiving benefits.

- Your retirement date and the start date of your Social Security benefits are not synonymous. You do not have to start your benefits just because you stop working. In many cases, it is better to use savings to supplement your income needs, and delay the start date of your Social Security benefits.

- Once you begin benefits, you can change your mind within the first 12 months if you are willing to repay what you received. If you are FRA or older you also have the option of requesting a voluntary suspension of your benefits to put them on hold. Then you can restart them later at a higher amount.

- If you have a previous marriage that lasted at least ten years, you are able to collect the higher of either your own benefit or a spousal benefit based on your ex's earnings record. (This will have no effect on your ex's benefit.)

- If you were born on or before 1/1/1954 then at your FRA you may be able to claim a spousal benefit first and then later switch to your own. If married, your spouse must have filed for their benefits already for this to work. If single but you have a previous marriage over ten years in length, this option may also be available to you.

It is easiest to understand these rules by looking at how they apply to you. Start by getting a copy of your Social Security statement.

Your Social Security Statement

If you are 60 or older, and not currently collecting benefits, Social Security will mail you an annual statement about three months before your birthday[9]. You can also access your Social Security statement online at any time (https://www.socialsecurity.gov/myaccount/).

Your statement provides an estimate of the benefits you might receive at age 62, at your FRA, and at age 70. Some people mistakenly look at their statement and think that if they don't begin benefits at 62, they must wait until 66, and that if they don't begin at 66 they must wait until 70. This is not true.

You can begin benefits anytime at 62 or later (age 60 if you are eligible for a widow or widower's benefit). The formula that determines what you get is re-calculated monthly, so each month you wait, your benefit increases.

Your statement also provides information on how your benefits are estimated and what assumptions are used. If you have not done so, get a copy of your statement, grab a cup of coffee (water or tea if you're not a coffee drinker) and read all four pages.

Here are a few key things to know:

- If you are closer to retirement, and have the majority of your working years behind you, the estimates you see on your statement will be more accurate.

- If you are farther away from retirement, or had many years of no or low earnings and now you are earning more, your final benefit amount is likely to be higher than what you see on your statement.

- The estimates on your statement are based on the assumption that you continue to work until you reach your Full Retirement Age and make about the same as you did in the year prior to your statement date.

- The amounts shown on your statement are stated in today's dollars. A cost of living adjustment will be applied to these. For example, if you are 62 today and your statement shows you will receive $1,000 at age 66, if inflation is 3% a year, your age 66 benefit amount with inflation adjustments will actually be $1,125 (assuming all other factors used to estimate your benefits, such as earnings between age 62 and 66, stay constant).

- If you receive a pension from earnings on which you did not pay Social Security taxes (most frequently this is from work for a federal, state or local government, non-profit, or foreign employment) the estimated benefit amount on your Social Security statement may be completely inaccurate. (This is due to two provisions: Windfall Elimination Provision (WEP) and Government Pension Offset (GPO). More information on these provisions is provided later.)

The most important decision you'll make is the age you begin your benefits, and if married, how you coordinate your claiming decisions with your spouse.

Age You Begin Benefits

Your Full Retirement Age (FRA) is assigned to you based on the year you were born. The FRA year of birth schedule[10] is listed below. Sometimes FRA is referred to as 'normal retirement age'. A lot of things hinge on your FRA.

When looking at the year of birth schedule, for each year, technically the year runs from a birth date of January 2 of that year to January 1 of the following year. For example, if you were born any day from January 2, 1955 to January 1, 1956 your FRA is the one listed after 1955, which would be 66 and 2 months.

If you were born January 1 of 1955 you are considered to have attained the age the year prior, so your FRA would be 66 (as according to Social Security you attained the age of 66 in 1954).

If you were born in 1937 or earlier, Full Retirement Age is 65.

- 1938: 65 and 2 months
- 1939: 65 and 4 months
- 1940: 65 and 6 months
- 1941: 65 and 8 months
- 1942: 65 and 10 months

- 1943-1954: 66

- 1955: 66 and 2 months

- 1956: 66 and 4 months

- 1957: 66 and 6 months

- 1958: 66 and 8 months

- 1959: 66 and 10 months

- If you were born in 1960 or later, Full Retirement Age is 67.

Your Social Security benefit amount is calculated relative to what you will receive at your FRA. There is a formula that lowers your benefit if you begin before this age, and a different formula that increases your benefit if you begin after this age.

The calculation is based on what is called your Primary Insurance Amount, or PIA. Your PIA is the monthly amount that Social Security calculates you will receive at your Full Retirement Age. All benefit calculations start with your PIA, then adjustments are applied. You can find detailed info on how your PIA is calculated in the Appendix.

Starting Benefits Before or After Full Retirement Age

If you claim benefits before your FRA, your PIA is reduced based on a formula that is recalculated monthly.

This formula is described below by Michael Kitces in his September 2009 issue of The Kitces Report[11]:

"If an individual chooses to begin Social Security retirement benefits before normal retirement age, then those benefits are reduced by 5/9ths of 1% for each month the benefits begin early, up to a maximum of 36 months. If benefits are started more than 36 months before normal retirement age, then each additional early month beyond the first 36 causes benefits to be further reduced, but only by 5/12ths of 1% per month."

In plain English, this means for each month you wait, you get a little more, or for each month you claim early, you get a little less.

Here are a few examples of how this formula affects you based on your year of birth:

- For someone with an FRA of 66, their age 62 benefit amount will be 75% of their age 66 benefit amount.

- From someone with an FRA of 67, their age 62 benefit amount will be 70% of their age 67 benefit amount.

If you want to get to 100% you'll wait until your FRA to begin benefits. If you want to get more than 100% then you'll wait even a bit longer.

Starting After Full Retirement Age

If you claim benefits after your FRA, delayed retirement credits apply, and for every month after FRA that you claim your PIA is increased by 2/3 of 1% per month[12] or 8% a year.

Delayed retirement credits offer significant protection against outliving your money, and for married couples can greatly increase the level of financial security for a sole surviving spouse.

Table 2-1 shows you how the Social Security reductions or delayed retirement credit increases affect two people, each with an FRA benefit amount of $1,000. One person has an FRA of 66, and the other has an FRA of 67.

Table 2-1. Benefit Amount after Applicable Reductions or Credits			
Born in 1943 - 1954		**Born in 1960 or later**	
Age	Benefit after reduction or credit	Age	Benefit after reduction or credit
62	$750	62	$700
63	$800	63	$750
64	$867	64	$800
65	$933	65	$867
66	$1,000	66	$933
67	$1,080	67	$1,000
68	$1,160	68	$1,080
69	$1,240	69	$1,160
70	$1,320	70	$1,240

Caution: Let's say you have an FRA of 66. If you go to apply for benefits at 66 and 6 months it is highly likely the folks at the Social Security office will try to give you a lump sum retroactive to what you would have received if you filed at your FRA, and then your ongoing benefit amount will be your FRA amount. By doing this, you will not receive your delayed retirement credit adjustment. When you file at odd ages if you want a higher ongoing monthly amount be insistent that your benefit amount be calculated based on your current age — not retroactive to how old you were many months prior.

Increasing your benefit amount is not the only reason to delay benefits. People who begin benefits before their FRA frequently get caught off guard by a rule that takes some of their benefits back if they go back to work.

Working and Collecting Benefits before Full Retirement Age

Occasionally I receive emails from readers who began their Social Security benefits early because they were laid off from work. A year or two later, they get a job opportunity and go back to work. At the end of the year they are shocked when they receive a notice that they owe some of their Social Security benefits back. This happens if three conditions apply:

- You are collecting your Social Security retirement benefit and,

- You have not yet reached your Full Retirement Age (FRA) and,

- Your income from earnings exceeds the Social Security's earnings limit (The earnings limit is $15,720 in 2015 & 2016. The year you reach FRA[13] this earnings limit is increased to $41,880. These limits are indexed to inflation.)

The amount of the reduction depends on how old you are relative to your FRA as follows:

- If you are younger than FRA for the full year, then benefits are reduced $1 for every $2 earned above the $15,720 earnings limit.

- If you reach FRA during the year, then benefits are reduced $1 for every $3 you earn above the $41,880 limit – if earned prior to reaching your FRA.

- There is a special rule for the year you reach FRA – you get a full Social Security check for any whole month you are FRA or older, regardless of yearly earnings. This means only earnings in months prior to you reaching FRA count toward the earnings limit.

- Once you reach FRA you can earn any amount and this reduction in benefits does not apply.

Bill and Jess provide a good example of how these rules can catch you off guard. They took Social Security in 2014 before they reached their FRA, expecting to have $20,000 a year of benefits plus self-employment income from a small business they started.

They earned $36,000 of net income in 2014 from their business. They received a notice to repay $10,260 of their Social Security benefits ($1 for every $2 over the 2014 earnings limit which was $15,480 - take $36,000 less $15,480 = $20,520 divided by 2), or receive no benefits until this amount was "repaid"[14].

If you find yourself in a situation where the earnings limit applies, don't panic. Your benefit amount will be recalculated to take into account months that you didn't receive benefits. The recalculation applies to the early retirement reduction factor that is used (this recalculation does not constitute a replacement of lost benefits).

For example, if you began receiving Social Security at 62 and exceeded the earnings limit in all of the next 48 months, the recalculation would restore your benefits to what they would have been at your age 66 without the early retirement reduction factor applied.

If you find yourself facing an unplanned early retirement, keep in mind even if you have not reached your FRA it may be to your benefit to use savings to supplement your income and delay the start of your Social Security so that when you find another job the earnings reduction will not apply. The exception to this may be if you have dependents eligible for a benefit based on your earnings record.

Chapter 3
Social Security for Marrieds

This is where the rules get complicated. Married couples have choices with their Social Security benefits that singles don't have. Studies show these choices are not well understood.

In a 2008 study titled When Should Married Men Claim Social Security[15], authors conclude,

"Most married men claim Social Security benefits at age 62 or 63, well short of the age that maximizes the expected present value of the average household's benefits. That many married men "leave money on the table" is surprising. It is also problematic. It results in much lower benefits for surviving spouses and the low incomes of elderly widows are a major social problem. If married men delayed claiming Social Security benefits, retirement income security would significantly improve."

Technically the last sentence of the prior quote should be changed to "If the higher earner of the two delayed claiming Social Security benefits, retirement income security would significantly improve."

The higher earner, whether that is the husband or the wife, has the ability to make choices that leave the couple in a more secure financial situation whether both should be long-lived or only one should be long-lived. It is not about being male or female; it is about developing a plan to get more as a couple.

Claiming strategies for married couples offer many possibilities because of two features of Social Security benefits that apply only to married couples:

1. **Spousal benefits** - As a spouse, you are eligible for a spousal benefit that is equal to 50% of what your spouse will get at their FRA, or your own benefit amount – whichever is higher. For those born on or after January 2, 1954, when you file you will be deemed to be filing for all benefits you are eligible for, and you will automatically be given the higher of either your own benefit, or if eligible, a spousal benefit. (In order to be eligible for a spousal benefit your spouse must have filed for their own benefit already.)

    a. For those who reach age 62 on or before January 1, 1954, depending on the relative ages of you and your spouse, you may be able to claim a spousal benefit for a few years, while letting your own benefit amount accumulate delayed retirement credits, and then switch to your own benefit at age 70.

    b. For example, when Sara reaches her FRA of 66, she could collect a spousal benefit of $1,086 (assuming 2% inflation by the time Sara reaches age 66 this will be $1,176) which is half of Sam's Full Retirement Age benefit of $2,173 as shown in Table 1-4, or she could collect a benefit of $1,313 based on her own earnings record. Initially, because her own benefit is larger, Sara thinks that is what she should take. In Sara's case, however, if she collects the monthly inflated spousal benefit of $1,176 at age 66, then when she reaches age 70 she can switch to her own age 70 benefit amount of $1,876.

2. **Widow/Widowers benefits** – Once you are both claiming Social Security when one spouse dies, it is the higher of the two Social Security benefit amounts that the surviving spouse continues to receive. The lower amount goes away. By planning to get the most out the highest earner's benefits, you can provide a significant survivor benefit to a spouse.

    a. In Sam and Sara's case, if Sam waits until age 70, he gets $3,104 per month. This higher monthly amount is then locked in as the survivor benefit for either spouse. If Sam collects at age 66, the lower $2,173 becomes the survivor benefit, and would represent a permanent lifelong reduction for either spouse, or both, who may be long-lived.

Note: The maximum spousal benefit payable is 50% of the earner's benefit at the earner's FRA. Spousal benefits do not participate in delayed retirement credits. If you are not eligible for your own benefit, but only for a spousal benefit, there is no benefit to waiting beyond your FRA to apply for your spousal benefit.

In order to use Social Security rules around spousal and widow/widower's benefits you have to learn about your ability to:

- File and suspend or request a voluntary suspension of benefits - which due to new Social Security rules will only work for the purpose of spousal benefit eligibility if you were born on or before 5/1/1950[16] and suspend benefits on or before 4/29/2016 (which is a Friday[17]). If you know people who fit this description pass the word along!

- File a restricted application – due to new laws signed Nov. 2, 2015, the restricted application option is only available to those born on or before 1/1/1954. Those born 1/2/1954 or later will not be able to restrict their application unless they are a widow/widower.

File and Suspend

Up until and including the day of April 29th, 2016 filing and suspending will allow your spouse to collect a spousal benefit while your own benefit continues to accumulate delayed retirement credits.

After April 29th, 2016 if you suspend your own benefits, then all benefits associated with your earnings record will also be suspended. (Note: You can only file and suspend once you are FRA or older – to be FRA by the end of April 2016 you had to be born on or before 5/1/1950.)

For example, suppose you and your spouse are both age 65 and your Full Retirement Age is 66, at which point you will receive $1,000 a month. After doing your homework you have decided you do not want to start benefits until 70.

If you reach age 66 on or before 5/1/2016 you can file and suspend your benefits, which then allows your spouse at their FRA to begin collecting a benefit of $500 a month (50% of your age 66 benefit amount). Since you have suspended your benefits they will continue to accumulate delayed retirement credits. When you reach age 70 you can begin your age 70 benefit amount of $1,320 (from Table 2-1,which in reality will have increased a bit more due to inflation adjustments.)

However this strategy will not work after April 29th, 2016. After April 29th, 2016 the only reason to suspend your benefit would be because you realize you claimed too soon; by suspending your benefit it will then continue to accumulate delayed retirement credits so you can start again later and get a higher monthly amount.

File a Restricted Application

Filing a restricted application continues to be allowed for widows/widowers. However, for married couples, in order to file a restricted application you must reach age 62 on or before January 1, 2016.

If married and you qualify for the restricted application it allows you to collect only your spousal benefit while your own benefit continues to accumulate delayed retirement credits.

(If widowed, regardless of your age you will be able to restrict the scope of your application to preserve your ability to switch benefit strategies later. The new law did not change this option for widows/widowers.)

For example, in Sara's case if she wants to collect a spousal benefit at her age 66, she will need to file a restricted application so she can collect the spousal benefit based on Sam's earnings record. As Sara attains the age of 62 before 1/2/1954 she can do this.

- If she does not file a restricted application she will be deemed to be filing for both her own and a spousal benefit and will automatically be given the larger of the two.

- If she does file a restricted application (after she reaches her FRA) she can choose which one to apply for, thus preserving her ability to later switch and apply for the other option.

Sara would choose the restricted application because then at age 70 she can file for her own benefit amount which will be higher based on her delayed start date.

Sara's sister Sally, who is a year younger, will not have the same options as Sara. When Sally goes to file, regardless of her age at time of filing she will be deemed to be filing for all benefits available and will be given the larger of either her own benefit, or, if married, a spousal benefit.

Note: regardless of your date of birth you do not have the option to file this type of restricted application before you reach your FRA unless you are a widow/widower.

Factoring all of this in is challenging. Larry Kotlikoff, Professor of Economics at Boston University, had this to say about it in his column on Forbes[18]:

> "Suppose the couple are the same age. The husband can apply for his spousal benefit in any of 48 months between 62 and 66. Same with the wife. They can both apply for their retirement benefits in any of 96 months between 62 and 70. But in all 48 months between 66 and 70 each spouse can suspend his/her retirement benefit collection and then restart it again later. This gives us 48 x 48 x 96 x 96 x 48 x 48 x 48 x 48 = 112.7 trillion combinations to consider.........my point is that we have a system that not only redefines complexity, but also defies understanding."

The rules are quite complex and Larry and several other industry experts have designed software to calculate your claiming options for you. If I were married, or eligible for a benefit on an ex-spouse's record, I would not even think about starting benefits without first running an analysis using such software.

Social Security Software and Calculators

It is impossible for this text to provide a comprehensive analysis of the different methods that online Social Security calculators use. Some tools use different methodologies than others, which can change the advice.

In addition, online tools are continuously being improved so at different times in the software development cycle, one tool may have more advanced capabilities than another, but that can change rapidly. I have provided a brief list of online resources below, listing the tools I am most familiar with for each category at the time of writing this.

From the Social Security Office

You can download a detailed Social Security calculator from the Social Security website; however, it will not evaluate claiming options for you and a spouse. You may find it useful for understanding the factors that affect your own benefit.

- https://www.ssa.gov/oact/anypia/anypia.html

For Free

SSAnalyze

There are several free online calculators that can help illustrate your benefit options, however the best one I have found is by Bedrock Capital Management. It is easy to use and lays out a recommended claiming plan for you.

When I input Sam and Sara's numbers, other than some minor differences related to rounding rules and the timing of the very first check, the numbers were in line with the projections I have used in this book.

- http://www.bedrockcapital.com/ssanalyze/

For a Fee

Maximize My Social Security

Maximize My Social Security was developed by Boston University economics professor Laurence Kotlikoff, software engineer Richard Munroe, and other professionals at Economic Security Planning, Inc., which markets personal financial planning programs.

This calculator covers all the Social Security claiming scenarios one might en-counter: retiree, spousal, survivor, divorcee, disabled, parent, and child benefits as well as calculations for the windfall elimination provision and government pension offset (which will affect you if you receive a pension from an employer who did not withhold Social Security tax from your earnings - such as a state employee.)

In the report provided by this software they do not project inflated benefit amounts; instead they show nominal amounts and discount them back to to-day's dollars using a real rate of return (the rate of return you expect to earn in excess of inflation).

- https://maximizemysocialsecurity.com/

For Financial Advisors

Social Security Timing®

This is the software I use in my practice. It was also used to calculate or dou-ble check most of the claiming options I have used in this book.

Social Security Timing® was developed by Joe Elsasser, CFP®, RHU, REBC, an Omaha-based financial planner. Joe is also the Director of Advisory Services for Senior Market Sales, Inc.

In his work as a financial advisor, Joe began testing a variety of Social Security calculator tools in search of a solution that would help his clients make the best decision about when to elect Social Security benefits. What he found was that every tool he tested, including the government's, was woefully incapable of providing a thorough analysis that took all of the election strategies for married couples into account.

For consumers this calculator provides a free look as to what is at stake be-tween a poor claiming choice and a planned claiming choice. It will list three strategies you may want to consider. To see the full strategy and the full report you will have to agree to be contacted by an advisor who subscribes to the full version of the software.

- https://www.socialsecuritytiming.com/

All three calculators provided a present value comparison of Sam and Sara's claiming options. Although each software program calculates present value in a slightly different way all three showed that for Sam and Sara, following a claiming plan as outlined in this book was worth more to them than claiming at their ages 66 and 62.

Even when using software it still helps to understand the rules so you know why one option might be preferable to another. Let's examine spousal benefits and widow/widowers benefits in greater detail and see how these items affect the total amount of income you and your spouse may receive.

Spousal Benefits

This is one area where I see misinformation coming out of the Social Security office on a regular basis. The rules are complex. Your average Social Security office worker may not know all of them. They are trained to deal with the most common situations.

If you have been married for at least one year (or if you have a previous marriage that was at least ten years in length and you have not re-married), you are eligible for a spousal benefit (assuming your spouse or ex-spouse is eligible for their own Social Security benefit).

Length of Marriage Rules

- 9 months – to be eligible for a survivor's benefit on your spouse's record

- 1 year – to be eligible for a spousal benefit

- 2 years – if your divorced spouse is 62, but has not yet filed, you must be divorced two years before you are eligible for a spousal benefit based on their record. If they have already filed for benefits there is no two year requirement to be eligible for the spousal benefit on an ex-spouse's record.

- 10 years – must have been married to claim on a spousal benefit on an ex-spouse's record

---

Even if you have your own earnings history, and your own projected Social Security benefit, some of you still have the ability to collect a benefit based on your spouse's (or ex-spouse's) record, and later switch to your own benefit, or vice versa. In a few pages in Table 3-1 you'll see how this works in Sam and Sara's situation.

The rules you need to know are:

- *If you were born on or before 1/1/1954 and you file for benefits before you reach your FRA*, you will forgo your ability to switch between spousal and your own benefits. Why? When you file early you are deemed to be filing for both your own benefits and a spousal benefit and Social Security will automatically give you the larger of the two. You cannot choose which to take.

- *If you were born on or before 1/1/1954, and you wait until your FRA to file*, you now have choices. You can file a restricted application and just collect a spousal benefit for a few years. This may be advantageous if your age 70 benefit amount would be higher, as you could switch over from a spousal benefit to your own at that point.

- *If you were born on or after 1/2/1954* regardless of what age you file you will be deemed to be filing for your own benefit and a spousal and will be given the larger of the two. You will not have the option to restrict your application.

You can increase your benefits by using these complex rules but you may need to go into the Social Security office armed with printouts from their own website to implement some of the choices available to you[19].

Let's put some of these rules in action by looking at Sam and Sara's choices.

Your Spouse and Collecting Benefits before Full Retirement Age

Sam and Sara, whose inflation-adjusted benefit amounts are in Table 1-4, provide a good example of how both spousal rules and widow/widower rules can be leveraged to your benefit.

Sam was born April 10, 1949, which makes him 66 in 2015. Sara was born January 2, 1953, which makes her 62 in 2015. They both have a Full Retirement Age of 66.

Sara did her own benefit calculations without considering spousal or survivor benefits. She now has a better understanding of how both spousal and survivor benefits work. She decides to redo her calculations one more time before sharing her numbers with Sam.

In Table 3-1 you see Sam and Sara's benefit amount based on Sam claiming at 66 and Sara at 62. In Table 3-2 you see an alternate choice they could make.

Table 3-1. Sam and Sara Claiming Social Security at 66/62						
Sam		**Sara**			**Present Value**	
Age	Benefit	Age	Own benefit	Widow benefit	PV discounted @ 3%	Cumulative sum of PV
66	$19,557	62	$10,920		$30,477	$30,477
67	$26,592	63	$11,136		$36,629	$67,106
68	$27,120	64	$11,364		$36,275	$103,381
69	$27,660	65	$11,592		$35,921	$139,302
70	$28,224	66	$11,820		$35,579	$174,881
71	$28,788	67	$12,060		$35,236	$210,117
72	$29,352	68	$12,300		$34,883	$244,999
73	$29,940	69	$12,540		$34,540	$279,540
74	$30,540	70	$12,792		$34,207	$313,746
75	$31,152	71	$13,044		$33,873	$347,619
76	$31,776	72	$13,308		$33,547	$381,166
77	$32,412	73	$13,572		$33,220	$414,385
78	$33,060	74	$13,848		$32,900	$447,286
79	$33,720	75	$14,124		$32,579	$479,865

80	$34,392	76	$14,400		$32,257	$512,122
81	$35,088	77	$14,688		$31,949	$544,072
82	$35,784	78	$14,988		$31,639	$575,711
83	$36,504	79	$15,288		$31,335	$607,046
84	$37,224	80	$15,588		$31,021	$638,068
85		81		$37,968	$21,653	$659,720
86		82		$38,724	$21,441	$681,161
87		83		$39,492	$21,229	$702,390
88		84		$40,284	$21,024	$723,414
89		85		$41,088	$20,819	$744,233
90		86		$41,916	$20,620	$764,852
91		87		$42,744	$20,415	$785,267
92		88		$43,608	$20,221	$805,488
93		89		$44,472	$20,021	$825,509

Table 3-2. Sam and Sara Claiming Benefits According to a Plan						
Sam		**Sara**			**Present Value**	
Age	Benefit	Age	Spousal benefit	Own/Wi dow benefit	PV discounted @ 3%	Cumulative sum of PV
66		62			$0	
67		63			$0	
68		64			$0	
69		65			$0	
70	$27,396	66	$14,112		$37,359	$37,359
71	$37,992	67	$14,388		$45,183	$82,543
72	$38,748	68	$14,676		$44,742	$127,284
73	$39,528	69	$14,964		$44,307	$171,591
74	$40,320	70		$22,512	$49,600	$221,191
75	$41,124	71		$22,968	$49,121	$270,313
76	$41,952	72		$23,424	$48,646	$318,959
77	$42,780	73		$23,892	$48,165	$367,124
78	$43,644	74		$24,372	$47,705	$414,829
79	$44,508	75		$24,852	$47,231	$462,060
80	$45,408	76		$25,356	$46,783	$508,843
<u>81</u>	$46,308	<u>77</u>		$25,860	$46,322	<u>$555,165</u>
82	$47,232	78		$26,376	$45,870	$601,035
83	$48,180	79		$26,904	$45,427	$646,462
84	$49,140	80		$27,444	$44,985	$691,447
85		81		$50,124	$28,585	$720,032
86		82		$51,120	$28,304	$748,336
87		83		$52,140	$28,028	$776,364
88		84		$53,184	$27,756	$804,120
89		85		$54,252	$27,489	$831,609
90		86		$55,332	$27,220	$858,829
91		87		$56,436	$26,954	$885,783
92		88		$57,564	$26,692	$912,475
93		89		$58,716	$26,433	$938,908

About the time Sam reaches 81 and Sara reaches 77 you can see the cumulative numbers in the far right column of Table 3-2 exceed the cumulative numbers at the same ages in Table 3-1. For each year they live past their ages 81/77 the Table 3-2 claiming plan becomes more attractive.

Table 3-2 shows Sam and Sara doing the following:

Sam files and suspends his benefits at age 66, near his 4/10/16 birthday. He will begin his own benefit at age 70.

Sara files for a restricted application for a spousal benefit based on Sam's earning's record at her Full Retirement Age (which is a few months before Sam's 70th birthday).

Sara switches to her own benefit at her age 70.

Sara decides to see how fast they would spend down their savings with each of these alternate claiming choices.

She adds up the amount of savings and investments that she and Sam have. It totals to $850,000. She assumes the investments earn 5% a year. She adds up their expenses including health care costs, property taxes, income taxes and everything else she can think of and determines they need about $80,000 a year to live on.

She runs some additional calculations to see how long their funds last (results shown in Table 3-3 and Table 3-4). She is shocked to see that if they begin Social Security at ages 66/62 then the year she reaches 88 they will run out of money. If they claim Social Security according to her alternate plan, then their funds last into the year she reaches 90.

Table 3.3. Sam & Sara's Savings After Withdrawal if They Start SS at 66/62 – inflation adjusted					Starting balance: $850,000
Sam's age	Sara's age	Income Needed	(less) combined SS benefit	(equals) gap that is withdrawn	Value after withdrawal, growing at 5%
66	62	$80,000	$30,477	$49,523	$840,501
67	63	$81,600	$37,728	$43,872	$836,460
68	64	$83,232	$38,484	$44,748	$831,298
69	65	$84,897	$39,252	$45,645	$824,936
70	66	$86,595	$40,044	$46,551	$817,305
71	67	$88,326	$40,848	$47,478	$808,317
72	68	$90,093	$41,652	$48,441	$797,870
73	69	$91,895	$42,480	$49,415	$785,878
74	70	$93,733	$43,332	$50,401	$772,251
75	71	$95,607	$44,196	$51,411	$756,882
76	72	$97,520	$45,084	$52,436	$739,669
77	73	$99,470	$45,984	$53,486	$720,492
78	74	$101,459	$46,908	$54,551	$699,238
79	75	$103,489	$47,844	$55,645	$675,773
80	76	$105,558	$48,792	$56,766	$649,957

81	77	$107,669	$49,776	$57,893	$621,666
82	78	$109,823	$50,772	$59,051	$590,746
<u>83</u>	<u>79</u>	$112,019	$51,792	$60,227	<u>$557,045</u>
84	80	$114,260	$52,812	$61,448	$520,377
85	81	$116,545	$37,968	$78,577	$463,890
86	82	$118,876	$38,724	$80,152	$402,925
87	83	$121,253	$39,492	$81,761	$337,222
<u>88</u>	<u>84</u>	$123,678	$40,284	$83,394	$266,519
89	85	$126,152	$41,088	$85,064	$190,528
90	86	$128,675	$41,916	$86,759	$108,958
91	87	$131,248	$42,744	$88,504	$21,476
92	88	$133,873	$43,608	$90,265	-$72,229
93	89	$136,551	$44,472	$92,079	-$172,523

In Sara's second set of calculations shown in Table 3-4 she can see that if they wait until a later age to start benefits they will spend down a fairly large portion of their portfolio in the next four years.

Table 3-4. Sam & Sara's Savings After Withdrawal if They Start SS Later – inflation adjusted					Starting balance: $850,000	Over/ Under
Sam's age	Sara's age	Income Needed	(less) combined SS benefit	(equals) gap that is withdrawn	Value after withdrawal, growing at 5%	Relative to Table 3-3
66	62	$80,000	$0	$80,000	$808,500	-$32,001
67	63	$81,600	$0	$81,600	$763,245	-$73,215
68	64	$83,232	$0	$83,232	$714,014	-$117,284
69	65	$84,897	$0	$84,897	$660,573	-$164,363
70	66	$86,595	$42,048	$44,547	$646,828	-$170,477
71	67	$88,326	$52,380	$35,946	$641,425	-$166,892
72	68	$90,093	$53,424	$36,669	$634,994	-$162,876
73	69	$91,895	$54,492	$37,403	$627,471	-$158,408
74	70	$93,733	$62,832	$30,901	$626,398	-$145,853
75	71	$95,607	$64,092	$31,515	$624,627	-$132,255
76	72	$97,520	$65,376	$32,144	$622,108	-$117,561
77	73	$99,470	$66,672	$32,798	$618,775	-$101,717
78	74	$101,459	$68,016	$33,443	$614,599	-$84,639
79	75	$103,489	$69,360	$34,129	$609,494	-$66,279
80	76	$105,558	$70,764	$34,794	$603,434	-$46,522
81	77	$107,669	$72,168	$35,501	$596,329	-$25,337
82	78	$109,823	$73,608	$36,215	$588,120	-$2,626
83	79	$112,019	$75,084	$36,935	$578,744	$21,699
84	80	$114,260	$76,584	$37,676	$568,122	$47,745
85	81	$116,545	$50,124	$66,421	$526,786	$62,896
86	82	$118,876	$51,120	$67,756	$481,982	$79,057
87	83	$121,253	$52,140	$69,113	$433,512	$96,290
88	84	$123,678	$53,184	$70,494	$381,169	$114,649
89	85	$126,152	$54,252	$71,900	$324,732	$134,204
90	86	$128,675	$55,332	$73,343	$263,958	$155,001
91	87	$131,248	$56,436	$74,812	$198,603	$177,128
92	88	$133,873	$57,564	$76,309	$128,409	$200,638
93	89	$136,551	$58,716	$77,835	$53,102	$225,626

She decides to see what happens if their investments earn a higher rate of return.

She determines that in order for them to have more funds remaining at her age 90, with the age 66/62 Social Security claiming choice their savings and investments would have to earn an annual rate of return after all fees and expenses of just over 8% a year.

While Sara has been researching Social Security options she has also been learning about investing. She attended an online class hosted by retirement researcher Wade Pfau. During that class she remembers that Wade showed that based on past market history approximately 1 in 3 retirees would not have earned a compound rate of return in retirement higher than 6% a year. (You can follow Wade online at retirementresearcher.com)

It was an eye opener for her to see that two investors could behave the same way and build the same diversified portfolios, but have very different out-comes depending on the time period that they live through.

She knows it is important to make decisions that put them in the most secure position regardless of what market conditions come along, and she knows earning a higher rate of return is not something that she and Sam can count on.

That's why one of the things Sara likes about claiming Social Security later is what things will look like at her age 75 - if they claim at 66/62 they will have $47,844 of guaranteed income; with the later claiming plan they will have $69,360 of guaranteed income at her age 75.

That is $21,516 more guaranteed income per year.

She looks at the inflation adjusted amount they'll need to live on at her age 75, which is $103,489. If they claim Social Security later a large portion (67%) of their expenses will be covered by their Social Security income. The thought of this makes her feel safer.

She realizes that following this plan can increase the amount of guaranteed income available to them later in life, without buying an annuity or any other investment product.

Sara is about to share her analysis with Sam when one other thought crosses her mind... what if Sam passes early? Before he reaches age 70? What happens then?

The short answer is that the decision will still benefit Sara as a survivor. The long answer is addressed by looking into how widow/widowers benefits work.

Chapter 4
Widow/Widower Benefits

Developing a plan on how and when to collect your Social Security benefits is not only smart, for married couples it can also be a cost effective way to provide life insurance.

If you've been married for at least nine months, these rules apply to you and your spouse, and can make a big difference for whichever one of you should be the longest lived.

The amount of a widow/widowers benefit depends on a few things:

- Whether the spouse who passed had started their benefits, and if so, whether they started before or after their FRA

- For the spouse who passes first, the amount of their benefit they were supposed to receive at their FRA (which I may refer to as your PIA or Primary Insurance Amount)

- Whether the surviving spouse has reached his/her full survivor benefit retirement age

Regarding the third bullet point, FRA for widow/widower's benefits is different than FRA for other benefit types. You cannot use the date of birth schedule for FRA retirement benefits to determine your FRA for survivor benefits. (I may refer to widow/widower benefits as survivor benefits.)

Instead you will need to look up the widow/widower FRA on the Social Security website[20], which is where I located the following data on FRA for survivor's benefits.

Sampling of FRA for Survivor Benefits

If you were born 1945 – 1956[21] your FRA for widow/widower benefit amounts is age 66. (For retirement benefits the age 66 FRA applies to those born 1943 – 1954.)

If you were born on or after January 2, 1957, your FRA for widow/widower benefits will be 66 plus a specified number of months.

If you were born on or after January 2, 1962 your FRA for widow/widower benefits will be age 67.

If you begin your widow/widower benefit before you reach your FRA for survivor's benefits you will receive a reduced benefit amount. There is no benefit to waiting past your survivor FRA to begin a widow/widower benefit amount.

Let's look at several potential scenarios and how a widow/widower's benefit amount would be affected.

If you start benefits before your FRA

- Your surviving spouse will receive a widow/widower's benefit that is the larger of what you were receiving or 82.5% of your PIA.

The 82.5% rule was put in place to protect a minimum benefit amount for a surviving spouse whose husband or wife began their own benefits early.

For example, if John has an FRA of 66 and was expected to receive $1,000 a month at his FRA, but he began benefits at age 62, he would receive $750. If John passes away his wife, Beth, if she has reached her survivor FRA, would receive a survivor benefit of $825 based on the 82.5% rule. (This amount would be further reduced if Beth had not yet reached her survivor FRA.)

If you start benefits after your FRA

- Your survivor is entitled to whatever you were receiving.

Again using John as an example, if he started benefits at 66 and is receiving $1,000 a month, his wife is entitled to the same $1,000 a month as a survivor benefit. If John passes at age 66 and Betty is 60 (and assuming she was born in 1956), if Betty chooses to begin receiving her widower benefit at 60, the $1,000 a month benefit will be reduced to $810 (based on looking up Social Security's Survivor FRA Chart by Year of Birth to see the reduction that applies based on the fact that she is claiming before her survivor FRA). Betty's survivor FRA is 66 so she would need to wait until her age 66 to receive the full $1,000 a month.

If John waited until age 70 to begin benefits his benefit would be $1,320 per month and this would then be the survivor amount Betty could receive. This amount would be further reduced if Betty began receiving it before reaching her own survivor FRA.

If you have not started your benefits yet and have not reached your FRA

- Your spouse can receive what you would have received at your FRA. (This amount can be further reduced if the surviving spouse has not yet reached their own survivor FRA.)

Let's say John passes away at 58, and has not started his benefits yet. If Betty were older than John (for example assume she is 66 and was born in 1950) she could begin benefits now and be eligible for the full $1,000 a month; which is the amount John would have gotten at his FRA. However if Betty had not reached her survivor's FRA, and had not begun her own benefits, and began her widower benefit early, then the amount would be reduced. For example, if Betty was age 60 she would receive $810 per month, not the full $1,000.

One of the unique options available to widow/widowers is the ability to claim a widow/widower benefit, then later switch to your own benefit, or vice versa, even if you claim before you have reached FRA. This means multiple potential claiming strategies should be examined before a surviving spouse decides which claiming plan is best for them.

If you have not started your benefits yet and you are FRA or older

- Your surviving spouse can receive the amount you would have received had you begun benefits at the time of your death. This applies if you delay the start date of your retirement benefits and pass away between your FRA and age 70.

This works because delayed retirement credits are applied to your PIA for the purposes of calculating the widow/widower's benefit amount even if you had not started your benefits yet.

Let's say John passes away at 69. He had not begun benefits. If he had his benefit amount would be $1,240. (This is his FRA benefit amount of $1,000 plus an 8% a year increase attributable to delayed retirement credits.) Betty can collect $1,240 at her survivor's FRA. (The amount will be reduced if she has not reached her survivor's FRA).

If you and your spouse have both already started your benefits

- The surviving spouse can continue the larger benefit amount, but not both.

In Sam and Sara's scenario, one possible future we must account for is Sam passing away early, and Sara living long. If Sam were to start benefits at 70, then pass away a year later, what happens?

Sara would be able to continue Sam's age 70 benefit amount, but her spousal benefit and her own benefit amount would go away.

How does this compare to their financial state if Sam had started benefits at 66?

- On a present value basis having Sam wait until age 70 to begin benefits is worth more than having him claim at 66, even if he passes at the end of the calendar year in which reaches age 70. (Numbers are shown in Table 4-1 and Table 4-2.)

- At Sara's age 75, she would have $44,508 of survivor benefit vs. $33,720 if Sam had started benefits earlier.

In the event of short longevity for either Sara or Sam, the Social Security plan put the surviving spouse in a better situation.

Sole Spouse Expenditures

Another thing to account for if you are running your own calculations: fixed expenses will often decrease at the death of the first spouse. Items such as health insurance premiums, transportation costs, and food are less for one than for two.

Table 4-1. Sam and Sara Claiming Social Security at 66/62, with Sam passing at 70

| | Sam | | Sara | | Present Value | |
Age	Benefit	Age	Own benefit	Widow benefit	PV discounted @ 3%	Cumulative sum of PV
66	$19,557	62	$10,920		$30,477	$30,477
67	$26,592	63	$11,136		$36,629	$67,106
68	$27,120	64	$11,364		$36,275	$103,381
69	$27,660	65	$11,592		$35,921	$139,302
70	$28,224	66	$11,820		$35,579	$174,881
71	$0	67	$0	$28,788	$24,833	$199,713
72	$0	68	$0	$29,352	$24,582	$224,295
73	$0	69	$0	$29,940	$24,344	$248,639
74	$0	70	$0	$30,540	$24,109	$272,748
75	$0	71	$0	$31,152	$23,875	$296,623
76	$0	72	$0	$31,776	$23,644	$320,268
77	$0	73	$0	$32,412	$23,415	$343,683
78	$0	74	$0	$33,060	$23,188	$366,870
79	$0	<u>75</u>	$0	<u>$33,720</u>	$22,962	$389,832
80	$0	76	$0	$34,392	$22,737	$412,569

81	$0	77	$0	$35,088	$22,522	$435,091
82	$0	78	$0	$35,784	$22,299	$457,390
83	$0	79	$0	$36,504	$22,086	$479,476
84	$0	80	$0	$37,224	$21,865	$501,341
85		81		$37,968	$21,653	$522,994
86		82		$38,724	$21,441	$544,434
87		83		$39,492	$21,229	$565,663
88		84		$40,284	$21,024	$586,687
89		85		$41,088	$20,819	$607,506
90		<u>86</u>		$41,916	$20,620	<u>$628,126</u>
91		87		$42,744	$20,415	$648,541
92		88		$43,608	$20,221	$668,761
93		89		$44,472	$20,021	$688,782

Table 4-2. Sam and Sara Claiming Benefits According to a Plan, Sam passes away at 70						
Sam		Sara			Present Value	
Age	Benefit	Age	Spousal benefit	Own/ Widow benefit	PV discounted @ 3%	Cumulative sum of PV
66		62			$0	
67		63			$0	
68		64			$0	
69		65			$0	
70	$27,936	66	$14,112		$37,359	$37,359
71	--	67	--	$37,992	$32,772	$70,131
72		68		$38,748	$32,451	$102,582
73		69		$39,528	$32,140	$134,722
74		70		$40,320	$31,829	$166,551
75		71		$41,124	$31,518	$198,069
76		72		$41,952	$31,216	$229,285
77		73		$42,780	$30,905	$260,191
78		74		$43,644	$30,611	$290,802
79		75		$44,508	$30,308	$321,109
80		76		$45,408	$30,020	$351,129
81		77		$46,308	$29,723	$380,853
82		78		$47,232	$29,433	$410,286
83		79		$48,180	$29,150	$439,436
84		80		$49,140	$28,865	$468,300
85		81		$50,124	$28,585	$496,885
86		82		$51,120	$28,304	$525,189
87		83		$52,140	$28,028	$553,217
88		84		$53,184	$27,756	$580,974
89		85		$54,252	$27,489	$608,463
90		86		$55,332	$27,220	$635,682
91		87		$56,436	$26,954	$662,636
92		88		$57,564	$26,692	$689,329
93		89		$58,716	$26,433	$715,762

Sara looks at the projected numbers for her as a survivor and is a little concerned that the present value of the later claiming plan does not surpass that of the earlier claiming plan until she reaches the age of 86.

She and Sam are both healthy, so she doesn't think there is a high likelihood that she would become a widow early. Nevertheless she decides to look up the probabilities associated with their life expectancies to see if she thinks having Sam delay until 70 makes sense for her even if he should pass away early.

What Do the Odds Tell You?

Figure 1-1 is a graph of life expectancy probabilities. It is based on a male and female, with the male age 66 today and the female age 62 today, and shows their respective probabilities of living to a particular age. Age is the horizontal axis.

Couples will want to focus on the "either" line. You can see at any age there is a higher probability that either of you will live to a particular age. This means when planning for two your resources have a potentially longer time horizon.

The crossover point, where the odds that neither of you is alive exceed the odds that one or the other of you is alive does not occur until almost 30 years out. What decisions do you suppose your 89-year-old spouse hopes you will make?

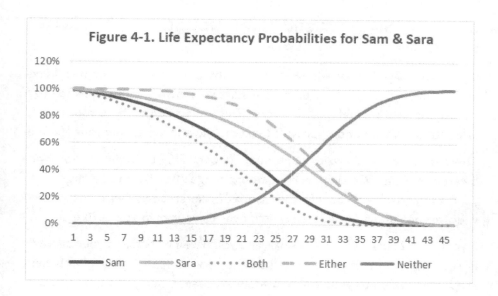

Figure 4-1. Life Expectancy Probabilities for Sam & Sara

Figure 4-1[22] shows the probability of Sam and Sara at their current ages of 66/62 living to a particular age, as well as the odds both, either, or neither of them should live to that age.

Suppose you are the betting type. You have a decision to make such as when to begin Social Security. You want to look at the odds to see which way you should bet your money.

- The odds tell Sara there is an 76% chance that one of them will still be here at what would be her age 86, 24 years from now.

- The odds tell her there is only a 4% probability that neither of them would still be here in 15 years.

You would think you would make the decision that would put you in a more secure position 76% of the time. Many people do not look at it this way. We have a tendency to place more value on a dollar of income today than a dollar of income in the future. That can hurt you in the long run.

After looking at this Sara realizes that 76% of the time maximizing that survivor benefit is going to work to their benefit.

Sara decides in this situation it would be a smart idea to play the odds.

If I'm the Survivor and Have Not Started My Benefits Yet

If you are the widow or widower, and you have not started your own benefits yet, you will have a choice. You can start your own, then later switch to a widow/widower's benefit, or vice versa. This is a situation where you want to calculate out which option provides you the most income over your lifetime.

There is no benefit to waiting past your survivor FRA to begin a widow/widowers benefit. If your own benefit amount at age 70 is likely to be larger than your widow/widower benefit then it may make sense to begin the widow/widower benefit early and then switch over to your own at age 70.

If your own benefit amount is small, and you have not reached your survivor FRA, in some cases it could make sense for you to file for your own benefit at 62, then switch to your widow/widower benefit when you reach your survivor FRA. Each case is different.

Keep in mind if you are filing for survivor benefits before you reach FRA the earnings test does apply to this benefit type.

And remember, when you go to apply you will need to restrict the scope of your application so you can specify whether you are applying for your own retirement benefit, or a survivor's benefit.

Chapter 5
Social Security for Divorcees, Singles & Dependents

Social Security for Divorcees

The same widow/widower benefits described for a spouse are available for an ex-spouse if you were married at least ten years and did not remarry prior to age 60.

In addition, spousal benefits are available on an ex-spouse's record.

To be eligible for a spousal (or widow(er)) benefit on an ex-spouse's record you must meet the following criteria:

- You had a previous marriage that was at least ten years in length

- You are currently unmarried (If you remarried after you reached age 60 you are eligible for a widow/widower's benefit on an ex, but you cannot collect a spousal benefit on an ex's record while you are currently married.)

- You are 62 or older (If your ex-spouse is deceased you are eligible for a widow/widower's benefit on their record as early as age 60.)

The Social Security representatives may not be able to advise you as to how to use ex-spouse benefits to your advantage. I saw this first hand with Mary.

Mary went to the Social Security office to inquire about claiming a benefit based on her ex-spouse's record. Social Security told her that if she did so the benefit amount would be about the same as if she claimed her own benefit and so they told her it probably didn't make sense for her to do this. They were right, and they were wrong.

All of the rules discussed on spousal benefits also apply for benefits based on an ex-spouse's record with one important difference. When married, your spouse must have filed for their own benefits in order for you to be eligible for a spousal benefit. When it is an ex-spouse this rule does not apply.

As long as your ex has reached age 62, even if they have not filed for their own benefits, you are still eligible for a spousal benefit (if they haven't applied for benefits yet you must be divorced for two years before you can apply for a spousal benefit on an ex-spouse's record).

The same rules about Full Retirement Age and date of birth apply:

- *If you were born on or before January 1, 1954 and file before your own FRA*, and your ex-spouse is 62 or older, you will be automatically given the larger of your own reduced benefit or a reduced spousal benefit. If you are receiving a reduced benefit it has nothing to do with your ex-spouse's age; the reduction is based on the fact that you are not yet FRA. If your ex-spouse is not yet age 62 then you are not eligible for the spousal benefit yet, so you would only be applying for your own benefit amount.

- *If you were born on or before 1/1/1954 and wait until your FRA to file*, you will be able to file a restricted application, claim a spousal benefit, and then later switch to your own benefit. An example of this is provided in Table 5-1.

- *If you were born on or after 1/2/1954* you will not have the option to file a restricted application for divorced spouse benefits unless your ex-spouse is deceased. For those born on or after 1/2/1954 when you file for benefits you will be filing for all benefits you are eligible for and will be automatically given the higher of your own benefit amount or an amount based on your ex-spouse's earnings record.

When you collect a benefit based on an ex-spouse's record it does not affect their benefit in any way. If you have an ex-spouse who collects benefits based on your earning's record, it will not affect your benefit in any way.

Mary was going to reach her FRA in a few months. Her benefit amount was going to be $1,366 a month at age 66. If she claimed a spousal benefit she would get $1,144 a month. Mary thought she should claim her own benefit amount because it was more.

A better choice will be for Mary to file a restricted application for a benefit based on her ex-spouse's record (Mary can do this because she was born prior to 1/2/1954), claim the $1,144 a month for four years, and then switch to her own age 70 benefit amount which (including 2% inflation and delayed retirement credits) would accumulate to $1,952 a month.

Regardless of whether Mary claims her own benefit or an ex-spousal benefit, if she has not remarried prior to age 60 when her ex-husband passes she will be eligible for a widower benefit.

In Table 5-1 you see both of Mary's options; Mary claiming her own benefit at 66, and Mary claiming a spousal at 66 and switching to her own at 70. In both cases, I assume Mary's ex passes away part way through the year that Mary reaches the age of 84 and so the benefit amount jumps up that year when she begins to receive the widower benefit.

Table 5.1. Mary's Social Security Claiming Options					
Mary's age	Mary's benefit	PV Cumulative Benefits Discounted @ 3%	Spousal benefit	Mary's Benefit at her age 70	PV Cumulative Benefits Discounted @ 3%
66	$16,392	$16,392	$13,728		$13,728
67	$16,728	$32,633	$14,004		$27,324
68	$17,052	$48,706	$14,280		$40,784
69	$17,400	$64,629	$14,568		$54,116
70	$17,748	$80,398		$23,424	$74,928
71	$18,096	$96,008		$23,892	$95,538
72	$18,456	$111,465		$24,372	$115,949
73	$18,828	$126,774		$24,852	$136,156
74	$19,200	$141,930		$25,356	$156,172
75	$19,584	$156,940		$25,860	$175,991
76	$19,980	$171,807		$26,376	$195,618

77	$20,376	$186,527	$26,904	$215,054
78	$20,784	$201,104	$27,444	$234,302
79	$21,204	$215,543	$27,984	$253,358
80	$21,624	$229,839	$28,548	$272,232
81	$22,056	$243,996	$29,112	$290,918
82	$22,500	$258,017	$29,700	$309,426
83	$22,944	$271,899	$30,288	$327,750
84	$32,624	$291,062	$35,744	$348,746
85	$39,996	$313,871	$39,996	$371,555
86	$40,788	$336,454	$40,788	$394,139
87	$41,604	$358,819	$41,604	$416,503
88	$42,432	$380,964	$42,432	$438,648
89	$43,284	$402,895	$43,284	$460,579

By the time Mary reaches age 72 her Social Security plan of claiming a spousal benefit first will have outperformed her initial choice which was to collect her own benefit at age 66.

Mary's sister, Marta, is divorced and in a similar situation. However Marta is five years younger than Mary. Since Marta was born after on or after 1/2/1954 Marta cannot file a restricted application. At whatever age Marta goes to file she will automatically be deemed to be filing for all benefits she is eligible for and will be given the larger of either her own benefit or a spousal benefit based on her ex's record.

Mary has one more sister, Marlene, who is six years younger than Mary. Marlene's husband passed away a few years ago. Because Marlene is a widow, even though she was born on or after 1/2/1954, she will be able to file a restricted application and collect a widow's benefit for many years. As Marlene worked most of her life, her own benefit amount at age 70 will be larger than her widow benefit, so Marlene will collect the widow benefit for several years and at age 70 switch to her own benefit amount.

Note: To claim a benefit on an ex-spouse's record be prepared to provide documentation such as copy of your marriage certificate and divorce decree.

Social Security for Singles

Conceptually, the Social Security formula was designed so that if you live to life expectancy you should get about the same amount no matter when you begin your benefits.

In an Investment News article titled Social Security and the Single Retiree, Mary Beth Franklin writes,

"Ironically, assuming that a single person lives to 80, it makes almost no difference when he or she begins drawing benefits. The cumulative lifetime benefits from Social Security will be about the same whether reduced benefits begin at 62, full benefits are taken at 66 or enhanced benefits start at 70."[23]

Using Sara as an example, if Sara lives to age 80, below are the total amounts she receives depending on what age she starts benefits (not including inflation adjustments):

- Age 62: $910 × 12 × 18 = $196,560

- Age 66: $1,214 × 12 × 14 = $203,952

- Age 70: $1,602 × 12 × 10 = $192,240

Today, people are living longer than ever. Advances in health care are occurring at a staggering rate.

If Sara lives to age 84, the answer changes:

- Age 62: $910 × 12 × 22 = $240,240

- Age 66: $1,214 × 12 × 18 = $262,224

- Age 70: $1,602 × 12 × 14 = $269,136

Additional factors such as interest rates and longevity should be part of the decision for singles.

A 2012 National Bureau of Economic research paper states:

"In general, women benefit more from delaying benefits, due to their longer life expectancies. For real interest rates of 0.8 percent or below, women maximize expected present value by delaying until age 70; on the other hand, even for a real interest rate of zero, men with average mortality risk maximize present value by delaying only until age 69. Delays of any length no longer increase present value for real interest rates above 3.5 percent for men and 4.2 percent for women."[24]

The interest rate component in the prior paragraph is important. The examples in this book where I have calculated present value have assumed a real rate of return of 1%. (Remember, real means the return amount in excess of inflation.)

If we move back into a higher interest rate environment where real interest rates are expected to be 4% or higher it will change the answer as to whether it makes sense to follow a particular plan or not.

Right now we are in a low interest rate environment and I ask singles to consider all of the following in regards to their Social Security decision:

- Will you work prior to reaching your Full Retirement Age? If yes, and if there is likelihood you will earn in excess of the earnings limit, then why mess with potentially having to repay benefits? Wait until you reach FRA to begin benefits.

- What story does your family health history and personal health history tell? Social Security provides inflation adjusted income as long as you live. The 84 year old you will have an increased level of security if the 62 year old you delays the start date of their benefits. Is this important to you?

- Do you have other savings you could use to supplement your income while delaying the start of your Social Security benefits? Sometimes you have no other options and must start benefits early. If you do have other options, have you explored them, and run a plan showing you how these choices play out over time?

- Do you have dependents that may be able to claim a benefit based on your record? Total family benefits should be considered when you evaluate your choices.

- Will you be eligible for a pension for work where you received earnings that were not covered by Social Security? If so, your Social Security benefit amount may be significantly reduced from what you see on your statement, or your spousal or widow/widower's benefit may be reduced.

There is an additional consideration which is that of risk. Immediate annuities are often a recommended investment for securing retirement income for singles. By delaying Social Security you are in effect buying an inflation adjusted annuity from Social Security.

In a Center for Retirement Research Paper one key finding says,

"Buying an annuity from Social Security is generally the best deal in town, especially in today's low interest-rate environment."[25]

If it's the best deal in town, make sure you take advantage of it before using your savings to go buy a lesser deal.

Social Security When You Have Dependents

With today's modern day family, it is more and more common to have parents of traditional retirement age who may still have dependent children, step-children or grandchildren.

If you...

- have a dependent child, step child, adopted child, grandchild or step-grandchild, or in some cases, illegitimate child who is under the age of 18 (or between 18 and 19 if they are a full time elementary or high school student)

- are caring for a child under age 16, and your spouse is deceased,

...then contact your Social Security office when you turn 62 to explore the total amount of family benefits you are eligible for.

For those who qualify for additional family benefits based on dependents, delaying Social Security may not be as advantageous. You'll need to evaluate your claiming choices side by side to see what choices lead to the most benefits for you and your family.

To dig into the rules I would recommend the current year edition of *Social Security & Medicare Facts* by Joseph F. Stenken J.D. CLU, ChFC® which provides great detail on family benefits, as well as details on all aspects of Social Security.

Chapter 6
When You Have a Pension from Work Not Covered by Social Security

To fund Social Security while working you and your employer pay a portion of your wages into the Social Security system. Social Security by nature is designed to replace a higher percentage of working income for low-wage earners than for high-wage earners.

If you worked for an employer who provides you a pension for years of work where you did not contribute to the Social Security system then based only on your Social Security covered earnings you may be a "low wage earner" and so the default provision would mean Social Security would replace a significant portion of your working income. In reality you may be a higher wage earner with earnings that were not covered under Social Security.

This situation began to be described as a "windfall". A modified set of formulas was designed to prevent someone in this situation from receiving excess Social Security benefits[26].

This provision of Social Security often affects fire fighters, law enforcement employees, postal workers and educators who work for government agencies or municipalities that have their own pension system and do not participate in Social Security.

For example, it affects teachers in fourteen states: Alaska, California, Colorado, Connecticut, Illinois, Kentucky, Louisiana, Maine, Massachusetts, Minnesota, Missouri, Nevada, Ohio, and Texas[27].

If you answer yes to any of the following questions, this section may apply to you:

- Did you work for a government agency (federal, state or local)?

- Did you work for an employer in another country?

- If yes to either question above, do you receive a pension from this government agency or employer in another country?

Note for Federal Employees

If you were a federal employee after 1956 and were covered under the Civil Service Retirement System (CSRS) this provision will affect you.

If you were a federal employee covered under the Federal Employees' Retirement System) (FERS) where Social Security taxes are withheld, this provision will not affect you.

There are two different rules:

Windfall Elimination Provision (WEP) – If you receive a pension from work that was not subject to Social Security taxes WEP may reduce your own Social Security benefit, and may affect your dependents benefits that are based on your earning's record (such as a spousal benefit).

Government Pension Offset (GPO) – If you receive a pension from work that was not subject to Social Security taxes then GPO may reduce the Social Security spousal benefit you receive (or benefit you receive as an ex-spouse), and may reduce the Widow/Widower's benefit you receive.

Windfall Elimination Provision

If you qualify for a pension[28] based on work where you had earnings not covered under Social Security, and you also had years of work with earnings that were covered under Social Security and qualify for a Social Security benefit too, then the Windfall Elimination Provision (WEP) may reduce the amount of Social Security that you qualify for.

Your Social Security statement will not reflect the deduction that may apply under WEP rules. Many people are caught off guard expecting to receive both their pension from government or foreign employment, and their full Social Security benefit. Instead, they receive a reduced Social Security amount.

The amount of the reduction depends on how many years of work you had that were covered under Social Security, and how much you made. If you have 30 or more years of substantial earnings for work covered under Social Security WEP will not affect you.

If the Windfall Elimination Provision does apply to you, a modified formula is used to determine the amount of your benefits.

For example, without WEP, your Social Security benefits are calculated by taking what is called your Average Indexed Monthly Earnings (AIME).

Then your AIME is used to calculate your PIA (benefit amount you receive at your Full Retirement Age) as shown in the formula below. (2015 numbers used):

- You take 90% of the first $826 of AIME

- You take 32% of the next $4,980 of AIME

- You take 15% of any amount over the $4,980[29]

You total those three numbers and add up to about what you would expect to get at your FRA.

If the Windfall Elimination Provision applies to you then a lower number is inserted to replace the "90%" that you see in the formula. The lower number to use is determined by how many years of work you have that were covered under the Social Security system.

In the Windfall Elimination Provision pamphlet[30] available on the Social Security website it shows you what number to insert into the formula based on how many years of covered work and earnings that you have had.

Let's look at an example. Assume Bob is making about $45,000 a year at age 60. Over his lifetime his average indexed monthly earnings (AIME) are calculated to be $4,525.

- 90% of the first $826 is $743

- 32% of the next $4,980 is $1,183[31]

- Those total to $1,926

Normally $1,926 would be Bob's PIA, or the amount he would expect to receive at his FRA.

Bob has worked for the state for the past 15 years. He will have a state pension and during his state employment he has not contributed to the Social Security system. However, prior to working for the state Bob had 23 years in the private employment sector and did participate in Social Security.

Bob has 23 years of what are deemed to be substantial earnings' years where he did participate in Social Security, and so in the formula the first bend point percentage is reduced from 90% to 55%.

- 55% of the first $826 is $454

- 32% of the next $4,980 is $1,183

- Those total to $1,637

Because of the WEP reduction Bob should expect $1,637 at his FRA, not $1,926.

You can use Social Security's online WEP calculator to figure out your own benefit reduction (https://www.socialsecurity.gov/planners/retire/anyPiaWepjs04.html).

The reduction in benefits can be as high as one half of the pension you receive, but not more than that. For example, if your pension was $2,000 a month, you could see your Social Security benefits reduced by $1,000 a month, but not by $1,100 a month.

Only pensions for work not covered under Social Security count - so if you had two pensions and one was from an employer where earnings were covered under Social Security that pension eligibility would not affect your Social Security benefits.

The WEP section of the Social Security website provides an excellent description of how this provision works and describes how the reduction formula works (https://www.socialsecurity.gov/pubs/EN-05-10045.pdf).

I say excellent because it explains the provision in language that you can actually understand. If you think WEP applies to you, I suggest you go online and read it.

If WEP does apply to you you'll need to use your reduced Social Security amounts to build your plan and to decide on a claiming strategy.

How does the Windfall Elimination Provision affect benefits for your dependents?

The Windfall Elimination Provision changes your primary insurance amount (PIA) as shown in the prior calculation. Dependent benefits are calculated using your PIA as a starting place. If the Windfall Elimination Provision affects your benefits it will also affect dependents' benefits that are calculated based on your record, however it will not affect a widow/widowers benefit that your spouse may receive after your death. The widow/widower's benefit is recalculated without WEP upon your death.

Dependents can also be affected if the dependent receives their own pension from work not covered under Social Security. This is covered under a separate rule called the Government Pension Offset.

Government Pension Offset

The Government Pension Offset (GPO) affects the benefit you might receive as a spouse, ex-spouse or widow/widower.

Same as the Windfall Elimination Provision, GPO applies if you receive a pension for years of work where you received earnings that were not subject to Social Security payroll taxes (also called OASDI "old age survivors and disability insurance"- the official name for Social Security).

If you are subject to the GPO rules your spousal or widow/widowers benefit will be reduced by two-thirds of the amount of your pension.

For example, if you will receive a pension of $900 a month that is from years of work that were not covered under Social Security then two-thirds of this amount (or $600) will be deducted from the spousal or widow/widower benefit that you would have otherwise received. If you were also eligible for a $1,600 widow/widower benefit, in this situation your widow/widower benefit would be $1,000 instead of the $1,600.

You can learn more on the Government Pension Offset page of the Social Security website. (https://www.ssa.gov/pubs/EN-05-10007.pdf)

If you are married and one of you is subject to GPO, you will need to factor this in before developing your own claiming plan. Assuming your spouse would be eligible for a full spousal or widow benefit would be incorrect if that spouse is subject to GPO.

If either WEP or GPO applies I would recommend using software that applies the relevant reduction factors and then calculates claiming choices for you.

Chapter 7
Fixing Claiming Mistakes, Taxes, Check Dates and Wrapping Things Up

If you don't have a claiming mistake to fix, skip to the Taxes section of this chapter.

Help! I Already Started Social Security. Can I Change My Mind?

Maybe you or your spouse already started Social Security. After reading through this chapter you may be thinking you could have followed a better plan. Joe Elsasser CFP®, developer of Social Security Timing® software, has the following four options on how you can fix things.

Option 1: Pay It Back

If you change your mind within the first 12 months of electing benefits, you can file a form 521 to withdraw the application and pay back any benefits. If benefits were received by auxiliaries, such as a spouse or children, those benefits would also need to be repaid. Once benefits have been repaid you are treated as though you never elected, which means you will not receive an actuarial reduction due to the original filing, and can file a restricted application for spousal benefits.

Option 2: Go Back to Work

If you are outside the 12-month window and decide you want to go back to work between the ages of 62 and Full Retirement Age (FRA), your benefits will be subject to an Earnings Test. The 2015 earnings test exempt amount is

$15,720 ($41,880 in the year you turn FRA). Social Security will withhold $1 in benefits for every $2 of earnings in excess of that amount. This is not a tax!

Let's say you elected benefits at 62 and were receiving an $1,800 monthly benefit (75% of $2,400) and now you want to go back to work at 63 earning $90,000 per year. $90,000 - $15,720 is $74,280. Divide that by two and the earnings penalty would be $37,140. Since that is greater than the total Social Security benefit of $21,600, you would not receive any Social Security for this period.

The reason we want to be very clear that the "earnings penalty" is not a tax is because Social Security would adjust the reduction on your benefits for each month in which you didn't receive a check due to the earnings test. If you actually received benefits for the 12 months you were 62, but then worked and did not receive any further benefits until age 66, SSA would go back to your record and adjust your benefit upwards. They will treat it as if you had originally elected at 65 instead of 62, so you would then begin receiving a check for $2,240 plus any Cost of Living Adjustments that had accrued.

Option 3: Voluntarily Suspend

There is another option for those who don't want to go back to work. Once you reach FRA, you can voluntarily suspend benefits. You simply need to call or visit a Social Security office and request a voluntary suspension. You can even call in advance of FRA with instructions to suspend at FRA.

Here's where it gets interesting. See if you can follow the math here. By electing at age 62, you basically reduced your monthly benefit to 75% of what you would have received if you had elected at FRA. By suspending benefits at age 66, you will increase your monthly benefit by 8% per year until age 70, for a total of 32%. So, if you increase 75% by 32% you get 99% (.75 x 1.32 = .99). In other words, you can take Social Security from 62-66, suspend from 66-70 and still get 99% of the benefit you would have gotten had you simply waited until Full Retirement Age.

This should not be viewed as a claiming strategy, only as a means for minimizing the damage of a mistake. There are several reasons one wouldn't want to elect at 62 with the intent of suspending at FRA. First, if you die between 62 and FRA, your widow/widower would be permanently stuck with a substantially reduced benefit. Second, you would forfeit any future option of claiming a restricted spousal benefit, because once you file for your own benefit, even if it is in suspension, your spousal benefit is reduced as if you were actually receiving your benefit. If your own suspended benefit is higher than your spousal benefit, you will not receive a spousal benefit.

Option 4: Maximize Benefits for your Spouse who has not yet elected

When you are married and one of you has already elected benefits and the other has not yet elected benefits, your best option is to identify the best of the remaining strategies for the spouse who has not yet elected.

The strategies to consider include the possibility of having the spouse who has already elected choose a voluntary suspension once they reach their FRA – however for couples this strategy is only available if the benefit is suspended on or before April 29th, 2016. After April 29th, 2016 if you suspend your own benefits then all benefits calculated based on your earnings record – including any spousal or dependent benefits – will also be suspended.

Real Life Example – I Fell For the Biggest Con There Is

George is one of the smartest clients I have ever worked with. He has numerous advanced degrees and enjoys digging into the details of decisions. He and his wife Chris came to see me at their ages 63 because they wanted an expert opinion on when he might be able to transition to part-time work.

A year prior he thought he had done all his homework on Social Security, and after seeking advice elsewhere, he had Chris begin her benefits at her age 62. She began receiving about $700 a month. He knew he would delay the start date of his own benefits.

He thought when Chris reached her FRA she would be able to switch and begin collecting a spousal benefit on his record, which would be about $1,100 a month. I had to be the bearer of bad news. Because Chris filed before she reached her own FRA, this switching strategy was not an option.

George's response was, "I fell for the biggest con there is. Free advice." He had gotten his earlier advice for free from a representative of a large well-known mutual fund company, and had followed the strategy they recommended. Since it had been more than twelve months since Chris had filed there was no way to undo the decision.

If they do nothing, then when George turns 70 and files for his own benefits Chris will automatically begin receiving an additional monthly amount of about $167 a month. Here's how that amount is calculated.

Chris's benefit at her FRA would have been $933. Her spousal benefit at her FRA would be about $1,100. $1,100 - $933 = $167. This is the amount her spousal benefit would have exceeded her own at her FRA. She will automatically begin receiving this spousal excess when her husband files for his own benefits (it will also be adjusted up for any cost of living adjustments that apply).

Their other option to "fix" the situation is to have Chris request a voluntary suspension of her benefits at her FRA, then resume her benefits at her age 70, which would bump her benefit up to about $900 a month.

When George reaches his FRA, he would collect a spousal benefit on Chris' record, then switch to his own benefit at his age 70[32]. George was both thankful for the fix, and frustrated as he realized this mistake would likely mean they would receive less total benefits than if he had been given the right advice initially.

I cannot emphasize the importance of doing a thorough analysis before you claim.

Taxes on Your Social Security Benefits

If Social Security is your sole source of income you will not pay taxes on it. If you have sources of income in addition to Social Security, up to 85% of your Social Security benefits may be subject to federal income taxes.

The formula used to determine the amount of taxes you might pay is not a simple one. It involves two steps; determining what your "combined income" is, and then applying the Social Security threshold amounts.

Determine What Your Combined Income Will Be

To determine if you will pay taxes on your Social Security benefits you must come up with an estimate of what you think your combined income will be.

Social Security considers your combined income to be approximately the total of your adjusted gross income (AGI) not including Social Security benefits, plus non-taxable interest, plus one half of your Social Security benefits. Roth IRA withdrawals are not included as income in this formula but municipal bond income is.

Apply Threshold Amounts

If your combined income exceeds the stated threshold amounts then a portion of your Social Security will be subject to taxation (these income threshold amounts are not indexed to inflation).

Married Threshold Amounts

If you are married and your combined income exceeds $44,000, then up to 85% of your Social Security benefits may be taxable.

If you are married and your combined income falls between $32,000 and $44,000 then up to 50% of your Social Security benefits may be taxable.

Single Threshold Amounts

If you file as an individual and your combined income exceeds $34,000, then up to 85% of your Social Security benefits may be taxable.

If you file as an individual and your combined income falls between $25,000 and $34,000 then up to 50% of your Social Security benefits may be taxable.

The way these threshold amounts are applied is with a formula that you can find in the IRS Worksheet[33]. This worksheet is part of the IRS Form 1040 instructions each year.

The formula can result in odd percentages of your Social Security being taxable - it is not simply 50% or 85%.

Let's look at an example so you can see the degree to which taxes can vary depending on the composition of your income.

For this example I used a free online calculator called How Much of My Social Security Benefit May be Taxed (https://www.calcxml.com/calculators/how-much-of-my-social-security-benefit-may-be-taxed). Please note - this calculator is only showing you the amount of tax due on your Social Security benefits based on your estimated marginal tax bracket that *you* input. It is not calculating your entire tax liability.

For that reason I used a separate online 1040 tax calculator to calculate the AGI, taxable income, and total federal tax liability[34].

Social Security Taxation Example

Let's look at a couple, both age 67, who are married and file jointly. One is collecting a spousal Social Security benefit while they both delay receiving their full age 70 benefit amounts. While delaying they are taking large IRA withdrawals. Here's a snapshot of their situation.

- $10k gross Social Security income

- $50k IRA withdrawal

- Combined income is $55,000 (which is in excess of the highest threshold amount for marrieds)

- Using the SS calculator 85% of their SS will be taxed, or $8,500

- They do not itemize deductions but instead use the standard deduction and exemptions

- Their AGI is $58,500

- Taxable income is $35,400

- Total tax due is $4,388

- After tax funds available to spend = $55,612

Now let's look at this same couple three years later. Both are age 70 and receiving their full Social Security amounts. Here's a snapshot of their situation.

- $40k gross Social Security income

- $20k IRA withdrawal

- Combined income is $40,000 (which is between the threshold amounts for marrieds)

- Using the SS calculator 10% of their SS will be taxed, or $4,000.

- They do not itemize deductions but instead use the standard deduction and exemptions

- Their AGI is $24,000

- Taxable income is $900

- Total tax due is $90

- After tax funds available to spend = $59,910

In both years the couple has $60,000 of gross income. However, after they are both 70, because a larger proportion of their income comes from Social Security their tax liability goes down.

If you want to gain a better understanding of how the Social Security taxation formula works search online for Prudential's *Innovative Strategies to Help Maximize Social Security Benefits* by James Mahaney. This brochure offers a detailed explanation of how the Social Security taxation formula works and why it should matter to you.

When you learn how to factor in taxes you'll see that many people have their withdrawal plan completely backwards. They take Social Security early and leave their retirement money alone, waiting until age 70 ½ when Required Minimum Distribution rules require them to begin taking withdrawals. From a tax perspective, for some people this can be one of the worst strategies. It is beyond the scope of this book to go into why, but I will be covering it in greater detail in an upcoming book.

When Will My Social Security Check Arrive?

Social Security retirement benefits (as well as disability and survivor benefits) are paid the month after you are eligible for them.

There are some interesting rules around eligibility. At age 62, if you turn 62 on the 1st or 2nd of the month, you will be eligible for benefits for that month, but if you turn 62 after the 2nd of the month, you won't be eligible until 62 and 1 month. This funky provision does not apply for other ages. Social Security puts it this way,

"Those born on the 1st are considered to have attained age 62 on the last day of the preceding month; those born on the 2nd are considered to have attained age 62 on the first day of their birthday month. Both could be entitled to benefits for the month of their 62nd birthday." [35]

For example, if you were born on the 15th of March and your FRA is 66, you will be considered to have reached age 66 and be eligible for a benefit the entire month of March even if you turn 66 in the middle of the month. However, if you were to file for benefits at 62, you would not be eligible until April, as according to the Social Security rules, you had not attained the age of 62 by March.

And if you were born on the first of the year? Here's what the Social Security website says,

"If you were born on the 1st of the month, we figure your benefit (and your full retirement age) as if your birthday was in the previous month. If you were born on January 1st, we figure your benefit (and your full retirement age) as if your birthday was in December of the previous year." [36]

Once you know what month you are eligible to receive a benefit you can determine what month to expect your first check (which will not actually be a check, but will be a direct deposit).

Using our example above, if this person born on March 15th filed at 62, his/her first month of eligibility would be April and they could expect their first check in May. However if they filed at 66 their first month of eligibility would be March and they could expect their first check in April.

Social Security checks are deposited on the second, third, or fourth Wednesday of each month, depending on your day of birth, according to the schedule below.

If you were born on the:

- 1 – 10th of the month, expect your Social Security check to be deposited on the 2nd Wednesday of each month

- 11 – 20th of the month, expect your Social Security check to be deposited on the 3rd Wednesday of each month

- 21 – 31th of the month, expect your Social Security check to be deposited on the 4th Wednesday of each month

Electronic Delivery of Social Security

As of March 1, 2013 Social Security no longer mails paper checks. There are two ways you can receive your benefits:

1. Direct deposit of your Social Security checks. This option puts the funds right into your bank account on the day they are paid. You don't have to worry about your check being lost or worry that funds will not get to the bank in time if you are out of town. Sign up or learn more online by searching for Frequently Asked Questions About Social Security Direct Deposit.

2. Direct Express® Debit Card - If you do not sign up for direct deposit, your benefits will be paid to you via Direct Express® debit card option. This card will work anywhere that takes Debit Mastercard®. You can also use your Direct Express® debit card to get cash back at the grocery store or to purchase money orders at the post office. Learn more at Direct Express® Debit Card (https://www.usdirectexpress.com/edcfdtclient/index.html).

What If Social Security Goes Away?

When I read online articles about Social Security claiming strategies I always find it fascinating to read the comments at the bottom. A number of them attempt to negate the information in the article by suggesting that Social Security won't be around and you should take your money and run.

Often the same people who say this have their money in the bank (backed by FDIC insurance which is backed by the U.S. Government), collect unemployment or other forms of benefits, or own U.S. bonds of some kind. So you are willing to count on the government for one form of sustenance but not another?

Yes, there will likely be changes to the Social Security system to make it viable for younger generations. Small changes like adjusting the Full Retirement Age up by one month can have a big impact on the overall system and a negligible impact on any one person. Those are the types of changes I foresee.

No one is required to stay in the United States. If you find another country which you believe provides more security, then go. That is your right. It is also your right to say whatever you wish as publicly as you wish. If you are near retirement age today, it is my right to think you are a fool if you are making your decision about Social Security based on a belief that it is going to go away.

Summary

The Center for Retirement Research offers a short brochure called The Social Security Claiming Guide. On the front page it says,

---

"A guide to the most important financial decision you'll likely make."

It is important to do analysis before you make this important and often irrevocable decision.

A smart Social Security decision that is integrated with the rest of your retirement plan can help provide a solid floor of guaranteed income.

The evidence is clear that everyone has something to gain from developing a Social Security plan, with married couples, or singles eligible for a benefit on an ex-spouse's record, potentially having the most to gain.

I think it is important to use software to advise you on your options. The rules are complex, and important nuances can easily be missed by trying to work through this decision on your own.

Be smart and design a claiming plan.

Appendix
How Are Your Benefits Calculated?

There is a three step process used to calculate the amount of Social Security benefits you are entitled to.

1. Use your earnings history to calculate your Average Indexed Monthly Earnings (AIME)

2. Use your AIME to calculate your Primary Insurance Amount (PIA)

3. Use your PIA and adjust it for the age you will begin benefits

The information you need is your own Social Security statement that provides your earnings' history, and the latest indexing factors, bend points, and wage limits which you can always find online.

Let's take a look at how it works.

Calculating AIME

Your Social Security benefit calculation starts by looking at how long you worked and how much you made each year. This earnings' history is used to calculate your Average Indexed Monthly Earnings (AIME).

The calculation works like this (an example is shown in Table A-1).

First - start with a list of your earnings each year since you worked

Your earnings history is shown on your Social Security statement, which you can now get online.

In Table A-1 actual earnings are shown in Column C. Only earnings below a specified annual limit are included. This annual limit of included wages is called the Contribution and Benefit Base (https://www.ssa.gov/oact/cola/cbb.html) and is shown as Max Earnings in Column H.

Second - adjust each year of earnings for inflation

Social Security uses a process called wage indexing to determine how to adjust your earnings' history for inflation. There are two main steps in the wage indexing process.

1. You take your earnings and create an index factor by dividing each prior year's earnings by the national average wages for the year you turn 60. You can fine each past year's published average wages at the National Average Wage Index page (https://www.ssa.gov/oact/cola/AWI.html).

2. You multiply each prior year's earnings by that year's calculated index factor.

Social Security provides online examples of how this works at their Benefit Calculation Examples page (https://www.socialsecurity.gov/OACT/ProgData/retirebenefit1.html).

I provide an example in Table A-1. In Table A-1 look at 1984's earnings of $21,000 in Column C.

The average earnings that year were $16,135, as shown in column D.

You take $44,888, the average earnings for the year this person turned 60 (in my example that is 2013 – wages are in bold italics) divided by $16,135, to get the Index Factor you see in Column E.

Multiply 1984's earnings by this index factor to get $58,422 that you see in Column F.

Because the wage indexing formula is finalized the year you turn 62 and indexed to wages for the year you turn 60, if you are not yet 62, your calculation to determine how much Social Security you will get is only an estimate.

Until you know average wages for the year you turn 60, there is no way to do an exact calculation. However you could attribute an assumed inflation rate to average wages to estimate the average wages going forward and use those to create an estimate.

Third – use your highest 35 years of indexed earnings and calculate a monthly average

Once you have indexed each year of past earnings, the Social Security benefits calculation then uses your highest 35 years of earnings to calculate your average monthly earnings. If you do not have 35 years of earnings, a zero will be used in the calculation, which will lower the average. In Table A-1 you see the highest 35 years in Column G.

Total the highest 35 years of indexed earnings and divide this total by 420 (which is the number of months in a 35 year work history). That is your Average Indexed Monthly Earnings or AIME.

Table A-1 How AIME Are Calculated

(no attempt to accurately follows rounding rules was made in these calculations)

A	B	C	D	E	F	G	H
Year	Age	Actual Wages	Average Wages From S.S.A	Index Factor	Indexed Wages After Cap	Highest 35 Years	Max Earnings
1971	18	1000	6497.08	6.909	6909	N/A	7800
1972	19	2000	7133.8	6.292	12586	N/A	9000
1973	20	3000	7580.16	5.922	17766	N/A	10800
1974	21	4000	8030.76	5.590	22360	N/A	13200
1975	22	5000	8630.92	5.201	26010	N/A	14100
1976	23	6000	9226.48	4.865	29196	N/A	15300
1977	24	7000	9779.44	4.590	32137	N/A	16500
1978	25	8000	10556.03	4.252	34024	N/A	17700
1979	26	9000	11479.46	3.910	35199	N/A	22900
1980	27	10000	12513.46	3.587	35872	35872	25900
1981	28	11000	13,773.10	3.259	35850	35850	29700
1982	29	18000	14531.34	3.089	55603	55603	32400

1983	30	20000	15239.24	2.946	58911	58911	35700
1984	31	21000	16135.07	2.782	58423	58423	37800
1985	32	22000	16822.51	2.668	58703	58703	39600
1986	33	23000	17321.82	2.591	59603	59603	42000
1987	34	24000	18426.51	2.436	58466	58466	43800
1988	35	25000	19334.04	2.322	58043	58043	45000
1989	36	25000	20099.55	2.233	55832	55832	48000
1990	37	25000	21027.98	2.135	53367	53367	51300
1991	38	27000	21811.60	2.058	55566	55566	53400
1992	39	29000	22935.42	1.957	56757	56757	55500
1993	40	30000	23132.67	1.940	58214	58214	57600
1994	41	36000	23753.53	1.890	68031	68031	60600
1995	42	37000	24705.66	1.817	67226	67226	61200
1996	43	38000	25913.90	1.732	65824	65824	62700
1997	44	39000	27426.00	1.637	63831	63831	65400
1998	45	40000	28861.44	1.555	62212	62212	68400
1999	46	41000	30469.84	1.473	60401	60401	72600
2000	47	42000	32154.82	1.396	58632	58632	76200

2001	48	40000	32921.92	1.363	54539	54539	80400
2002	49	40000	33252.09	1.350	53997	53997	84900
2003	50	40000	34064.95	1.318	52709	52709	87000
2004	51	43000	35648.55	1.259	54145	54145	87900
2005	52	45000	36952.94	1.215	54663	54663	90000
2006	53	46000	38651.41	1.161	53423	53423	94200
2007	54	48000	40405.48	1.111	53325	53325	97500
2008	55	50000	41334.97	1.086	54298	54298	102000
2009	56	44000	40711.61	1.103	48514	48514	106800
2010	57	44000	41673.83	1.077	47394	47394	106800
2011	58	46000	42971.61	1.045	48052	48052	106800
2012	59	48000	44321.67	1.013	48614	48614	110100
2013	60	45000	*44888.16*	1	45000	45000	113700
2014	61	45000	44888.16	1	45000	45000	117000
2015	62	-	44888.16	1			118500
					Sum of G:	1,919,040	
					Divided by 420 = AIME:	$4,569	

Fourth - calculate your PIA

Once you have calculated your AIME, you plug that number into a formula to determine your Primary Insurance Amount, or PIA.

The Social Security benefits formula is designed to replace a higher proportion of income for low income earners than for high income earners.

To do this, the formula has what are called "bend points". These bend points are adjusted for inflation each year.

Bend points from the year you turn 62 are used to calculate your Social Security Retirement Benefits. Below I show 2015 bend points. It works like this:

- You take 90% of the first $826 of AIME.

- You take 32% of the next $4,980 of AIME.

- You take 15% of any amount of AIME over $4,980.

You total those three numbers.

The result is your Primary Insurance Amount, or PIA.

Your PIA is rounded to the next lowest dime, and your benefit amount is rounded to the next lowest dollar. (Technically your PIA is calculated, rounded to the next lowest dime, then any inflation adjustments are applied. That number is then rounded to the next lowest dime. Then any increase or decrease based on age is applied. That number is then rounded down to the next lowest dollar.)

You can see historical bend points and the current year's bend points on the Bend Formula Bend Points page (https://www.socialsecurity.gov/OACT/COLA/bendpoints.html) of the Social Security website.

If you are not yet 62, your benefit calculation is only an approximation, as you do not yet know what the final bend point amounts for the year you turn 62 will be. You can use an estimated inflation rate to approximate future year's bend points to develop a relatively accurate projection.

If we take the AIME of $4,569 calculated in Table A-1, below you can see how the AIME is plugged into the bend point formula to calculate the PIA.

- 90% of the first $826 of AIME = $743.40

- 32% of the next $4,980 of AIME = $1,197.76

- 15% of any amount of AIME over $4,980 = 0

- Total $1,941.16. Rounded down to the nearest dime is $1,941.10 and down to the nearest dollar $1,941. This person's PIA, which is the amount they would receive at their FRA, is $1,941 [37].

As wage indexing and bend point numbers are finalized the year you turn 62, many people wonder if their PIA can change after they reach age 62. The answer is yes.

There are two things that will affect your PIA after you reach age 62.

1. **Higher Earnings** - Earnings in years between age 62 and 70 that are higher than one of the 35 highest earnings' years previously used in the formula will change your AIME which is used in the PIA formula.

2. **Inflation** - Your PIA will be adjusted by the same Cost of Living Adjustments applied to people who are already receiving Social Security benefits. You can see historical Cost of Living Adjustment Rates on the Social Security website (https://www.ssa.gov/news/cola/automatic-cola.htm). Note: this is not the same adjustment that is used to index wages for inflation.

Word of caution: the biggest reason people get the wrong answer when they run their own calculations on when to begin Social Security is because they take the numbers off their statement and do not properly apply inflation adjustments.

Once your PIA is calculated it is adjusted up or down based on the age you begin benefits. This determines the actual benefit you receive and these age related adjustment were covered in the Social Security Basics section of this book.

Footnotes

[1]https://www.congress.gov/bill/114th-congress/house-bill/1314/text#toc-HB-0761134CD9140EF87627EA34FDDB1E1, H.R. 1314 – Bipartisan Budget Act of 2015, Section 831, Closure of Unintended Loopholes. The new laws change two aspects of Social Security claiming; the restricted application and the voluntary suspension of benefits (often referred to as "file and suspend").

[2] https://www.ssa.gov/OACT/FACTS/

[3] http://www.ssa.gov/oact/cola/colaseries.html

[4]https://www.ssa.gov/news/press/basicfact.html, Social Security Basic Facts, October 13, 2015

[5] In Table 1-2 and all tables that show potential future savings' balances, it is assumed withdrawals occur at the beginning of the year, then the rate of return is applied, and the end of year balance is what is shown.

[6] Because of the Social Security rounding rules, if you try to replicate the calculations and apply a 2% increase on your own, you may not get exactly the same answer.

[7] Sara determined this 7% by increasing the rate of return on her savings in her projections simultaneously for both the early and late claiming scenarios. The return had to be increased to 7% or greater before the projected savings balance (by the end of the year she reached 89) for the early claiming plan surpassed that of the age 70 claiming option.

[8] Many finance folks recommend using a "real" rate of return, which is the return you might expect to earn in excess of inflation. A good proxy for this would be the rate on long-term TIPS (Treasury Inflation Protected Securities). However, since Sara has already inflated her benefit amount and is now taking the present value of that inflated income stream, she should use the nominal rate of return she expects to earn on safe investments. For example if you expected you could earn 1% above inflation,

and you expect inflation to be 2%, your real rate of return is 1%, and your nominal rate of return is 3%.

[9] Social Security is also mailing a paper statement to individuals under 60 at 5 year increments, so at age 25, 30, 35, 40, 45, 50, 55, and then each year at age 60 and beyond.

[10] According to the Social Security office "If your birthday is on January 1st, we figure your benefit as if your birthday was in the previous year. If you were born on the 1st of the month, we figure your benefit (and your full retirement age) as if your birthday was in the previous month." -Source: http://www.socialsecurity.gov/retire2/agereduction.htm

[11] The Kitces Report, 9/09, by Michael E. Kitces, MSFS, MTAX, CFP®, CLU, ChFC, RHU, REBC, CASL, CWPP™, verification can be found in the Social Security Handbook section 724.1.A

[12] For those born in 1943 or thereafter. For those born prior to 1943, the formula provided a lesser increase for delaying. Data in the Social Security handbook section 720.3.C.

[13] The year you reach FRA, only earnings prior to you reaching FRA count toward this limit. To learn more specifics see How Work Affects Your Benefits, SSA Publication No. 05-10069, ICN 467005, January 2015. You can find it online at http://www.ssa.gov/pubs/10069.html#a0=2.

[14] 2015 Social Security and Medicare Facts, by Joseph F Stenken, J.D. CLU, ChFC® Q. 223 Can a person lose some or all Social Security benefits by working?

[15] http://crr.bc.edu/briefs/when-should-married-men-claim-social-security-benefits/, by authors Steven A. Sass, Wei Sun, and Anthony Webb, March 2008, Center for Retirement Research at Boston College

[16] If you attain FRA on the first day of the month for Social Security purposes it is as if you attained the age in the prior month. According to the rules someone who attains the age of 66 on 5/1/2016 would technically reach FRA in April 2016 and would be eligible for suspending benefits under the old rules. In addition, one attorney, Avram Sacks, makes an incredibly valid case of interpreting the law to mean that anyone who reaches FRA as late as August 2016 would still be eligible to file and suspend under the old rules. You can read his interpretation here: Alternative Interpretation of Bipartisan Budget Act of 2016.

[17] Technically the law specifies that the new rules regarding suspending benefits begin 180 days after the enactment date of this law which was 11/2/2015. By our and other industry expert calculations that means you could still suspend benefits under the old rules on 4/30/2016 – but as that is a Saturday I have chosen to use the 4/29/2016 date throughout this text. In addition, one attorney, Avram Sacks, makes an incredibly valid case of interpreting the law to mean that anyone who reaches FRA as late as August 2016 would still be eligible to file and suspend under the old rules. You can read his interpretation here: Alternative Interpretation of Bipartisan Budget Act of 2016.

[18] Thomas Jefferson Is Rolling in His Grave -- A Rant on Social Security's Complexity, 8/6/12, Forbes Online

[19] Visit the Retirement Planner: Benefits For Your Spouse section of the Social Security website at https://www.socialsecurity.gov/planners/retire/yourspouse.html if you need references to help you follow your claiming plan.

[20] https://www.ssa.gov/planners/survivors/survivorchartred.html, Social Security Benefit Amounts For the Surviving Spouse By Year Of Birth

[21] I am simplifying the calendar years. Keep in mind the "born 1st of the year" rules; someone born 1/1/1967 is considered to have been born in 1966 for purpose of these rules.

[22] Graph derived from spreadsheet developed by David E. Hultstrom of Financial Architects, LLC, using white collar mortality numbers for Sam/Sara.

[23] http://www.investmentnews.com/article/20120226/REG/302269976 , 2/26/12

[24] The Decision to Delay Social Security Benefits: Theory and Evidency, by John B. Shoven, Sita Nataraj Slavov, NBER Working Paper No. 17866, February 2012

[25] http://crr.bc.edu/briefs/should-you-buy-an-annuity-from-social-security/ , Center for Retirement Research of Boston College, Should You Buy an Annuity From Social Security, May 2012

[26] See Social Security Handbook section 718 Windfall Elimination Provision (WEP)

[27] OLR Research Report, Sept 7, 2006, https://www.cga.ct.gov/2006/rpt/2006-R-0547. htm

[28] Lump sum distributions from plans where earnings were not subject to Social Security are not covered in this section. If you want to dig read Retirement Planning for

Workers Impacted by the Windfall Elimination Provision at https://www.onefpa.org/ journal/pages/apr15-retirement-planning-for-workers-impacted-by-the-windfall-elimination-provision-.aspx

[29] The cut off numbers ($826 and $4,980) are called "bend points" and they are indexed to inflation.

[30] https://www.socialsecurity.gov/pubs/EN-05-10045.pdf , SSA Publication No. 05-10045 ICN 460275, August 2015

[31] Take Bob's AIME of $4,525 less the first bend point amount of $826 to get $3,699 that falls into the second bend point formula. 32% of $3,699 is $1,183 (rounded down to the nearest dollar).

[32] George can do this because he reached the age of 62 on or before 1/1/2016. The option to restrict an application to only spousal benefits will not be available for those turning 62 on or after 1/2/2016. In addition, Chris must suspend benefits on or before 4/29/2016. If she were to suspend benefits after this point, then George would not be able to receive a spousal benefit while Chris's benefit was suspended.

[33] https://apps.irs.gov/app/vita/content/globalmedia/social_security_benefits_worksheet_1040i.pdf , Social Security Benefits Worksheet – Lines 20a and 20b, 2014 Form 1040

[34] I used the online 1040 tax calculator at DinkyTown.net for the 2015 year to calculate the AGI, taxable income and total tax due. Calculator is at: https://www.dinkytown.net/java/Tax1040.html

[35] https://www.ssa.gov/policy/docs/ssb/v62n3/v62n3p51.pdf

[36] https://www.ssa.gov/planners/retire/agereduction.html

[37] I'll be honest. I don't know if I have applied the rounding rules accurately to every part of this formula – nor to all the calculations in this book. I have decided it is not material to the outcome.